Here and There

Here and There
(or the Padre looks in)

Memoirs of Canon Grant Ockwell

Copyright © Atticus Communications Ltd 2009

All rights reserved. No part of this publication may be reproduced or transmitted in any form or by any means, electronic or mechanical including photocopying, recording or any information storage or retrieval system, without prior permission in writing from the publishers.

The right of Grant Ockwell to be identified as the author of this work has been asserted by him in accordance with the Copyright, Designs and Patents Act 1988

First published in the United Kingdom in 2009 by
Atticus Communications Ltd

ISBN 978-0-9562604-0-6

Foreword

CANON GRANT OCKWELL'S MEMOIRS – 'HERE AND THERE'

Grant Ockwell retired in 1981 and began his association with St John's, Westbourne, in the same year. He and Muriel were already, therefore, 'part' of the Diocese of Chichester (even though living in Portsmouth Diocese) before I first arrived in 1982. So it came as something of a surprise to me to realise that Chichester has simply been his 'retirement' diocese! I just assumed he had always been part of the scene. But of course this quarter of a century has itself been a significant part of Grant's life and ministry.

These pages are a fascinating series of recollections of a long, rich and varied life: I hope they will be widely read and provide a model for others to record the memories that might otherwise be lost. This does of course highlight the importance of listening attentively and respectfully to the voices of age, not sufficiently regarded in our present society. From a theological point of view, what we are celebrating in any Christian life is above all the work of God's grace seen in the context of a particular life. The specificity and beauty of every individual life tell us something unique about God's purposes and can teach us much for our benefit and the better living of our own lives. God wastes nothing; neither should we.

These memoirs have a particular resonance for me, being formerly, like Canon Ockwell, a priest of the Diocese of Southwark. Personal associations apart, however, the sensitive reader will find in these pages not only a record of a faithful life and ministry, but also an overview of many significant events of the 20th and early 21st centuries. I am deeply grateful to Fr Grant for having put pen to paper.

✝John Cicestr

The Rt Revd John Hind, Bishop of Chichester February 2009

Preface

Many times our four children, Andrew, Timothy, Rachel and James, have tried to persuade me to commit the story of my life and my adventures to paper, but I have always resisted their requests because surely hardly anyone would wish to read them when the task was done. However, at the end of many years of retirement I found myself with little to do and time on my hands so I thought I would engage in some personal 'occupational therapy' by writing my memoires. So here they are.

'Here and There' tells of my long life, and I am grateful to my children for their help and encouragement in getting me going and in preparing the text for publication. Without their help 'Here and There' would never have seen the light of day.

Grant Ockwell

The beginning

According to legend a Cockney is someone born within the sound of Bow Bells – the bells of Saint Mary le Bow in Cheapside. If the legend is true then I am a Cockney, since I was born in the London Hospital on April 22nd 1912. We lived then in North London, at South Tottenham, and I spent all my boyhood days there. Tottenham has several rather surprising historical connections. All Hallows, its ancient parish church, is situated in Bruce Grove and the adjoining railway station is named Bruce Castle, so there must have been a castle there at some time and Robert Bruce had associations with this part of the world.

Some time in the 18th Century some boys from a bible class held at the parish church, formed a cricket club called the Hotspur Cricket Club and later on formed a football club as well. Both cricket and football clubs were called "Hotspur" because the boys had been learning about the exploits of Sir Henry Percy who apparently fought in battle at the age of 14 and was nicknamed Harry Hotspur because he was a reckless fighter, very hot headed, and wore his spurs when on horseback. The Percy family were once great landowners in the Tottenham area and as Earls of Northumberland are remembered to this day by the name Northumberland Park, and there is also an inn called The Northumberland Arms. Now we have a famous football club named Tottenham Hotspur, known to everybody as The Spurs. As a boy I used to go and watch the Spurs, and still follow their fortunes.

My father, Thomas James Ockwell, was born in the village of Cricklade in Wiltshire, a place where he told me one could jump over the river Thames because the source of that great river is not far from there. The name Ockwell is unusual in most of England but in the county of Wiltshire it is comparatively common and can be seen on war memorials and grave stones. At the present time there is a glove making company in Cricklade running under the name of Ockwell, though it has, as far as I know, no direct connection with our family. Recently (2007, a time of exceptional flooding) television news bulletins featured an item that the River Ock had overflowed its banks at Abingdon, some 15 miles from Cricklade, towards Oxford. The Ock is a tributary of the Thames, and I wonder if the modern City of Oxford took its name from "Ock's Ford".

My grandfather on my father's side died before I was born and I have little knowledge of him, though we have traced the family tree back some 400 years. My father in his youth was apprenticed to a saddler and harness maker, and at the age of about 18 left where he was born and went to work in London. He used to travel from home to the city by tram, six days a week, to where he was employed in the heart of the City working among horses. These were used to pull Royal Mail vans (this being before the age of motor vehicles) and as a small boy I was often taken to London and City Road in Moorgate, to see the mews and the rows of horses in their stalls. Horses were still kept there until the first year of the Second World War and subsidised by the Government in case the Army needed them.

My father could do anything with a horse, and I remember as a boy walking with him along the towpath of the River Lea when a horse drawing a barge refused to go under a low bridge. He put his arm round the horse and talked to it, then led it calmly to the other side. Some folk have this sort of gift and I recently read a book called 'The Horse Whisperer' which reminded me very much of this incident. My father retired just before the outbreak of war in 1939.

My mother came from Essex, near Romford. How she met my father I do not know, and I have only hazy memories of her family. I wonder now why I never did ask questions when she was alive and she would have been able to answer them. She died in 1962 leaving me with memories of things I wish I knew more of today.

Soon after he came to London my father married and had three children, but his first wife died leaving him with the children then aged seven, five and three. How he managed at that time I do not know, but some while afterwards he met and married my mother and she started her married life caring for the three children now aged nine, seven and five. She then had five children of her own. The first one, George, died at birth, the second, Lily, died aged eight months. Hilda, Rosa and I followed at roughly three-year intervals. Hilda, or Queenie as she was known, died of tuberculosis aged fifteen. I remember going to visit her in a large, bleak sanatorium. In those days the hope of a cure for tuberculosis was just 'fresh air', and if you could afford it you were sent to the Swiss Alps or somewhere similar. If you couldn't, the only option was a sanatorium somewhere in the country, where all the beds were on an open veranda, and if it rained or snowed a Mackintosh cover was put over the bed.

After she was married, my mother's sister, Agnes, emigrated to Canada and she sent me magazines for my birthday and at Christmas to show me something of life in that faraway land. We still have cousins in Canada and I was able to visit them in 1982. Rosa, while she was still alive, kept in touch with our cousins over there, and after she died her daughter Frances kept up the correspondence. Recently Frances received a letter enclosing another letter, which was one from Queenie, written from the sanatorium, in 1922, about six weeks before she died. In it the 15 year old girl had written, "I cannot write any more because my hands are so cold. Do you know, I went to have a drink of water from the beaker on my locker and the water was frozen solid."

When it became obvious that Queenie would not get better, my father brought her home to die. The day she died he came home from work at midday, and when my mother opened the front door, she exclaimed with surprise, "Why have you come home early?" He replied, "I just felt I had to." Queenie died that afternoon at 4pm, and I remember taking my farewell of her. On the day of the funeral, April 1st, 1922, we awoke to find several inches of snow, and because of it, train services were disorganised, and members of the family coming from the West Country arrived late and missed the funeral service in church.

The Christian faith of my father suffered a severe setback during this period. He had lost his first wife, and then lost two infant children from his second marriage, before the death of Queenie, aged 15. He then suffered from a mugging in which he was robbed of his week's wages, and later on a burglary at his house. All these things proved too much to take. In the light of this it is perhaps remarkable that my sister Rosa went on to become a most faithful Sunday School teacher and remained a real stalwart of the Church all her days, and I went on to train for the Sacred Ministry. It is good to be able to say that my father recovered his faith and knelt by my side at the altar for the very first time when I was about 20. He became a sidesman and a member of the Parochial Church Council at his local parish church.

When the First World War began I was aged two and a half, and I have vivid memories of air raids by German Zeppelins. At such times policemen on bicycles would ride by with placards bearing the warning "Take cover". On one occasion I was pulled into a shop doorway by my father in order to take shelter from a raid. Once we were staying at Westcliff-on-Sea when the noise of many aircraft approaching could be heard. For some reason we were all outside and many people were looking skywards thinking the planes were all 'ours'. A man called out, "There are 72 of them," and at that moment a terrible raid began. They were German aircraft, not British.

Not far from where we lived was Saint Ann's Hospital and it was requisitioned by the Army for war casualties, and it became a common sight to see convalescent soldiers in their blue suits wandering around for exercise. Rationing of food did not start until 1917, which meant that whenever a supply of sugar, butter or other scarce foodstuffs arrived the word would go round and everybody rushed to get a share. In the Second World War rationing was introduced at the beginning and everything we needed was much better organised.

The war of 1914/18 took its terrible toll of human life, but at last the day came when an armistice was signed and peace was proclaimed at 11 o'clock on the 11th day of the 11th month – November 11th 1918. The vicar came into our school to tell us the good news, so no more school that day! At the age of six, I remember the tremendous excitement, relief and joy, and the crowds thronging the streets. The evening of Armistice Day turned into a real London 'pea souper', which did its best to dampen the celebrations. Hardly any families had escaped bereavement, and my brother, who was some years older than I, was called up and served in the Army. He suffered a terrible injury to his face and was invalided out, scarred and disfigured for the rest of his life.

Dense fog in London was then a fairly common occurrence. At the time we had regular visits from a blind piano tuner, and on one particular foggy day he came to tune the piano as usual. My mother opened the door and exclaimed, "I didn't expect to see you today because of the fog"- completely forgetting that for him one day was much the same as any other.

From the house where we lived in South Tottenham we could see and enjoy the grounds of St Ann's nursery and also sample the produce - cucumbers, tomatoes etc. The nursery no longer exists and the site is now covered by rows of houses.

Those were the days when the muffin-man came round ringing his bell, and the baker called with an assortment of loaves – round tin, long tin, square tin, Coburg, farmhouse, cottage loaf and so on. Today bread is marketed in a very plain form so there is no question of 'bagging' the crust from the Coburg, or the top of a cottage loaf, as we children used to do. The cockle and mussel man went by, as did the coalman, at different times and on different days. One day when my mother was going out she said to me, "If the window cleaner comes, I've left sixpence (2 1/2p) for him on the mantelpiece."

Milk was delivered long before we were up in the morning, and the custom was to hang a milk can on a nail in the porch the night before. The milkman would come and fill it with a pint of milk and later on in the morning he would return to see if we needed any more. On my uncle's farm in Wiltshire they milked the cows by hand at 4 o'clock in the morning, then took the churns to Minety Station by horse and cart, to catch the milk train to Paddington. In later years the churns were put on a small wooden platform by the road and collected by lorry. Nowadays the cows are milked automatically and a tanker comes and connects directly to the bulk tanks in the dairy.

I haven't many noteworthy memories of school life – just one or two incidents stand out. The headmaster always wore a straw boater – very common at that time – and every morning he would come in, take off his hat, put it on the desk and say, "Good morning boys". One morning for some reason he left the classroom and I picked up his hat, put it on and then swept it off, exclaiming "Good morning boys". Unfortunately for me, a member of the class had a water bottle in his hand and the top of the hat hit the neck of the bottle causing quite a large hole in the straw. I pushed the straw back out and did my best to make the hat look undamaged, placed it back on the desk and kept quiet, feeling more than a little guilty.

Eventually my conscience got the better of me and I went to the headmaster and told him what I had done. He told me off, of course, but was really extremely kind. I then offered to pay for a new one, though exactly how I could have done so from my meagre pocket money I really don't know. After that, if ever the town Luton was mentioned he would always turn to me and ask, "What is Luton famous for?" At that time it was famous for straw hats (long before any connection with motorcars) and Luton Town Football Club is still nicknamed 'The Hatters'.

The only other thing I recall from my school days is my endeavour to make long distance swimming records, and I have several certificates, and a silver medal for swimming two miles that I gained at the age of 14.

Almost every child attended Sunday School, and I went each Sunday at 10.00 am and 3.00 pm. Every Summer we had an outing to the sea, and the train from Saint Ann's Station had to pull up twice in order to pick up the large numbers of teachers and children. As I grew up the family became more and more involved with activities at the Parish Church, and I joined the scouts and the tennis club, went on parish rambles and joined in carol singing at Christmas time.

Before Queenie died, the three of us, Queenie, Rosa and myself, went to Henshaw's Academy of Music. Queenie learned the piano and Rosa and I the violin. Queenie accompanied Rosa and both progressed extremely well. But when Queenie died it meant there was no one to accompany Rosa, so it was decided that I should take lessons on the piano. I continued playing the violin and the piano for many years, and played regularly while a student. After I was ordained there seemed no opportunity to continue with the violin, though the piano was different and I could, and did, stand in and play the piano or the organ in an emergency. In later years arthritis in my hands made piano playing impossible, but Rosa continued to play the violin and gave concerts well into her eighties. Now my grand-daughter Sophia possesses Rosa's violin and is quite an accomplished musician.

As a family we were in the habit of going away for a summer holiday to places like Yarmouth, Margate, Folkestone and Eastbourne. There was a system, long since gone, called 'Cooking and Attendance' which meant people 'let' rooms and cooked whatever food the holidaymakers provided. It worked well because it meant we got the food we enjoyed most. My father was a great swimmer and would be up swimming in the sea long before breakfast. Not all summers though were wonderful, with endless sunshine, as some people declare they were in 'the good old days'. One year in Eastbourne the weather was so bad that we went to the theatre in the afternoon to a circus performance, and when we left at the end the floods were so deep that my father had to take off his socks and shoes and carry us children through the water. Those were the days!

Radio was very much in its infancy and called 'the wireless' because there were no wires connecting it to the outside world (except for an outdoor aerial which stretched the length of the garden) unlike the telephone, which had masses of wires visible on telegraph poles, and which were connected to the receiver in one's household. My father would sit for hours with a primitive crystal radio set and try to get a sensitive spot on the crystal. When he did, everybody and everything had to be quiet – not even a newspaper could be rustled – so that the sound of 'London calling' and the chimes of Big Ben could be heard in the headphones. One day our next door neighbour came round and invited us to come to their house and hear the first loudspeaker that any of us had ever heard. I am sure that had I, or anyone else, dared to forecast today's miraculous communications - television, space travel, mobile phones and so on – people would have declared it impossible and probably have suggested there must be something wrong with the speaker's head.

When I was 14 the opportunity came for me to attend Ponders End Technical School, an establishment that was an outstanding innovation in England at that time. As well as ordinary classrooms there were engineering workshops with lathes, a forge, and many other facilities not normally found in a school. I enjoyed working with my hands, but endured subjects like geometry and trigonometry and didn't take kindly to the massive amount of homework set for us.

On leaving school at the age of 16, I applied to be accepted as a Youth in Training, a form of apprenticeship, with the General Post Office. The GPO, or the Post Office, was responsible for all telephone systems at that time. I had a few months to wait before starting my new life and got a job working in a calculating machine factory, the calculating machines being an early form of computer. It was no doubt a very good baptism for going out into the big wide world as there were some very rough diamonds working there who took the rise out of me when they discovered I was a Scout and went to church.

One day a particularly nasty sort of man happened to be working alongside me and he started talking about the war days, meaning the war of 1914-18. He went on to say that his Padre had been a wonderful bloke and had gone on to win the Military Cross. I told him my vicar at home had been an Army chaplain and had also won the Military Cross. He asked me his name and then realised it was the same man who had been his wartime Padre. He was so excited about it and asked me to tell the vicar I had met him.

I promised to do so and went on working at the lathe, turning out screws. A few minutes later he sidled up to me and said: "You know you promised to tell the vicar about me? Well you won't tell him what I'm like now, will you?" He was just like a naughty child, this large, uncouth, foul-mouthed man, but he obviously had a conscience. I did tell the vicar, and reported back to the man, and he was just like that little child again. I left the factory soon afterwards, so never knew whether he changed his ways.

The Post Office informed me I was to report to Clissold Telephone Exchange at Dalston Junction, not far from Moorgate in the City, and I worked there for two years. Automatic telephone systems had just been developed, and until that time all telephones and telephone exchanges were manually controlled with rows and rows of telephone operators enquiring, "Number please?" and then connecting up the required line. I was as happy as could be and seemed all set for a career in the Post Office telephone department, but due to the influence of our most splendid curate at that time, one Fred Finch, at St Ann's, our parish church, I began to think more and more that I was doing the wrong job and felt called to be a priest. All sorts of difficulties faced me – how could I leave my job? How would I manage for money? Would anyone consider me good enough? and so on.

The thought persisted and just would not go away, but I decided it was impossible for me and I'd better forget it. Then I happened to attend a special service in St Paul's Cathedral and the preacher took for his text "He that puts his hand to the plough and looks back is not fit for the Kingdom of Heaven". It was just as if he was talking directly to me and I knew that I must persevere with my efforts towards ordination.

The first thing to do was to try and save some money, so I bought a second hand bicycle for just 10 shillings (50p). Not much of course, but quite a lot of money at that time, and each day I cycled to work to save the fare For lunch I had just a roll and butter and spent nothing unless it was absolutely necessary and saved every penny I possibly could. The time came when I felt I could go and see the vicar and consult him about any possible way I could pursue my objective. He outlined the difficulties, but finished by saying it might be possible for me to be accepted for training by the Society of the Sacred Mission at Kelham Theological College, near Newark on Trent in Nottinghamshire, though it would all depend on a number of things – I would need letters from him, from my most recent headmaster, the Post Office, my scoutmaster and so on, all testifying to my good behaviour and general suitability. Anyway, the vicar said I could write off and ask to be considered. This I did and eventually received a letter asking me to go to Kelham for a selection weekend in March 1930.

I then had to confess to my parents what I had been doing and my intention for the future. My mother was quietly thrilled, but my father took the practical view and gave me a lecture. "Giving up a good job", he said. "No real prospect for the future, and what happens if you don't make the grade?" Sound advice, but my mind was made up, so off I went to visit Kelham. I am a little hazy about my weekend there, but there were interviews, sharing with the students in the life of the college and joining in the worship in the chapel. The chapel was modern but had an austere beauty, which lent itself to quiet and to prayer. On returning to London I had to sit back and wait, but eventually the postman brought a letter bearing the postmark 'Newark on Trent', and it contained the longed for information that I could go for my first term on September 30th 1930. I can feel the joy and excitement in my bones over that letter even now.

So I had to go about handing in my notice to the GPO and tell the members of staff I would be leaving at the end of August. Surprisingly, they were very understanding and when the time came, wished me well. My sister Rosa had encouraged me all along and was a great help and support. Members of the youth group at St Ann's presented me with various tokens of good wishes for the future, and at last the day came for me to leave home and take up residence at Kelham on September 30th 1930.

I haven't much idea what I did on the day I left to catch the train from Kings Cross, except that I sat at the piano and played, and half hummed the words of the hymn "Just as I am". I added a verse not found in the original version: "Just as I am, young strong and free, to be the best that I can be, for truth and righteousness and Thee, O Lamb of God, I come."

Kelham

Arriving at Kelham with about 20 other new students, we were shown round and told where to sit in Chapel, in the refectory and where to sleep. Like most people I had terrible bouts of homesickness and longed for the very first holidays which seemed as though they would never come. In our first term we studied such things as English, ancient history, elocution, Latin and Greek. The general course of studies at the beginning lasted about two years, and at the end of it there was an exam called QE - short for Qualifying Exam. After the exam a notice was put up on the notice board, which said: "The following have satisfied the examiners." So heart in mouth I had to look and see whether my name was on the list or whether my career at Kelham had come to an untimely end. Imagine my relief and joy when my name appeared and I could start the four-year course of Theological studies.

Tennis Captain 1934

Life at Kelham was physically and mentally strenuous. Football in the winter and cricket or tennis in the summer were compulsory. I enjoyed taking part in these activities and later on, in 1934, I was appointed tennis captain. We also produced plays and revues of various sorts. The Rector of Averham (the village next to Kelham) was an enthusiastic theatre-goer and producer, and he had built a miniature West End of London theatre in his garden, complete with footlights and fittings just as they would be in a London theatre. We were allowed to use it, and many times I enjoyed sharing in productions there. I played the violin in the small orchestra we formed, and performed on the drums in the dance band section when we accompanied musical plays. Altogether enjoyable additions to the years of study, and I have very happy memories of it all.

Kelham String Septet

The football 1st 11 played to a very high standard, and against the 2nd 11 of local professional teams such as Nottingham Forest, Notts County, Chesterfield and Mansfield Town. It was the custom to entertain the visiting team to tea after the match and show them round the college and the chapel, and I once heard one of the visiting players say: "All this for an outworn superstition". At the time of writing, the outworn superstition has lasted another 75 years!

Herbert Kelly, the founder of the Society of the Sacred Mission, and therefore of Kelham Theological College (the "Old Man", as he was known), was giving a lecture and said:, "If when you are preaching or teaching someone says 'Ah, how true, how true', you will know you have probably been talking nonsense." One of the students piped up immediately with, "Ah, how true, how true".

Kelham Chapel, as I have mentioned, was very modern, indeed almost austere, but also beautiful and with an atmosphere conducive to prayer and meaningful worship. Everything was done in perfect order, and all students had to attend choir practice on Saturday mornings and rehearse the hymns and setting for the service next morning. Great care was taken in training the servers, and even when one had been doing such duty for several years it was still required that a rehearsal was necessary. The result was a very high standard of service and ritual, and one that without doubt resulted in a similar high standard of ministering in church by Kelham trained priests. Quite often people have remarked of former students, "You can tell he's a Kelham man".

The austere beauty of Kelham Chapel

Every so often someone of note would come and stay for a few days and give a talk in the common room. One of these was T S Eliot, the poet, who would read his own poetry and in doing so make it all come alive in a way I had never heard before. Senior students were chosen as representatives and attended a Student Christian Movement conference at Swanwick, a large conference centre in Derbyshire, and this proved for me a most enjoyable and profitable experience.

It was also the custom for various Dioceses of the Church of England to run summer schools throughout the month of August. These were held at different seaside resorts and free places were offered to theological students. Summer schools provided a wonderful holiday for young people from inner city parishes, and consisted of outdoor activities, games, sports, and of course worship. In my last year at Kelham, a notice appeared offering places at Southwark Diocesan Summer School at Seaford in Sussex. Two of my friends and I volunteered to go there in August and we set forth accordingly for the south coast.

We had no idea what we were letting ourselves in for, and on arrival sat on a bench by the sea and decided it was a bit foolish of us to have become involved. Then one of my companions said he would go and find the school, have a look round and come back and report. On his return he told us all was well, bathing costumes were hanging out of the windows to dry, peals of laughter could be heard and young people were playing cricket and tennis and obviously enjoying life to the full. So off we went, and there followed one of the happiest weeks of my life. The combination of worship, fun and interesting and instructive lectures made for a wonderful atmosphere, and in many cases provided lasting foundations for friendship. Years later, our eldest son, Andrew, met his future wife Eileen at one of Southwark's summer schools. For me this was to be the beginning of a lifelong association with the Diocese of Southwark.

During my student years I spent many holidays at Osborne's Farm near Minety in Wiltshire, staying with my aunt Emily and uncle John. My aunt, my father's sister, was a lovely warm and gentle person, and life on the farm was a delight. I much enjoyed helping with the haymaking, milking the cows, harnessing the horse and cart, and also playing cricket with my cousins. The farm was almost entirely self-supporting. All fruit and vegetables were grown alongside the farmhouse, and my uncle kept pigs and chickens, and rabbits were plentiful. My cousins were bell ringers at Minety Church and everyone joined in all kinds of Church and village activities.

One might be tempted to think that life on a farm, miles from anywhere, would be rather dull and not very fulfilling for young people. Not a bit of it. My cousin's children had all sorts of hobbies, and joined in all kinds of activities in the village. Margaret had a most wonderful collection of butterflies, Kathleen learned upholstery and could be found busy working at upholstery in one of the sheds, Ken was interested in model aeroplanes and actually built, in the barn, an aeroplane big enough for him to fly in. It actually flew, but only as far as the hedge, and the plane did not fly again! After I was married and with a young family, we spent many happy holidays down on the farm.

At summer school I met Eric Eyden who was curate at St Matthew's Church, New Kent Road, Elephant and Castle in South London - about a mile from London Bridge. Eric told me he was leaving his parish in the near future and his vicar was looking for his successor so would I be interested? Indeed I would, as it sounded exactly the sort of place I felt called to serve. The system in the Church of England is that a man at the end of his training serves his Title in a parish for 12 months as a deacon, and after another exam and post ordination training he is ordained priest. First the vicar has to be satisfied that a possible new assistant would be suitable for the parish and if so inform the Bishop. All being well the official wheels would start to turn and the day of the ordination would be fixed. So I had to make an appointment to see the vicar, Arnold Turner, and I went to the Vicarage and met him and his wife. Both made me very welcome and said that I should offer myself for the vacancy of assistant curate. From then on, while still a student at Kelham, all the official procedures began to happen and I was looking forward to starting my new life at St Matthew's in the Diocese of Southwark.

The last of my days at Kelham went swiftly by, and with the other students about to be ordained we went into retreat, and then after a special service in Kelham Chapel were sent on our way.

So we went home to get items of clothing, robes etc and all the other bits and pieces needed to become a lodger in a bed-sit, in my case in Trinity Square, just off the Borough High Street, near St George's Church. This is a famous Church, mentioned in the writings of Charles Dickens, and that part of London is full of history. Just up the High Street there is still the George Inn, London's only surviving galleried coaching inn, which was also used as a theatre in days gone by. Shakespeare had his lodgings nearby and almost certainly went to watch plays there. Just round the corner is the Tabard, the starting point for Chaucer's pilgrimage to Canterbury in 1388 and the subject of his famous Canterbury Tales.

All of London south of the Thames is now in the Diocese of Southwark, though until the end of the 19th century it was in the Diocese of Winchester. It seems very odd nowadays to think of this part of London being grouped with rural Winchester, but for many centuries the Diocese of Winchester stretched from the River Thames to the coast of Hampshire and included the Isle of Wight. Interestingly, in 1952, when I became Vicar of St Andrew's Surbiton, I found a plaque in the porch commemorating the consecration of the Church by a Bishop of Winchester. How the Bishop managed to get around a Diocese of such an enormous area, before the advent of trains and motorcars, makes one's mind boggle. Until fairly recently Bishops wore breeches and gaiters, a relic no doubt from the days when they travelled on horseback.

Ordination

Three days before the ordination service, which was to be held in Southwark Cathedral, candidates attended a rehearsal and then went into retreat at the Diocesan Retreat House at Carshalton in Surrey. The Cathedral itself is a very lovely building hard by London Bridge and is dedicated to St Mary Overie, meaning St Mary-over-the-Bridge. Old London Bridge was on the river level – even in the river - and in comparatively recent times the road and the bridge were raised to allow the river to flow underneath it. This has the effect of leaving the Cathedral below the bridge standing on the bank of the Thames, and there is a long flight of steps leading down from the highway to reach the entrance below. The Cathedral is full of historical reminders and commemorative tablets and memorials of all the wonderful people who have served God in that particular place, and inside the building there is an atmosphere of prayer and worship reminding one of its long history.

It is not hard to imagine the excitement, mixed with feelings of trepidation, as I and the other ordinands made our way by train from Carshalton to London Bridge Station on the day of the ordination. Crossing the road and down the steps to the Cathedral, wearing a clerical collar for the first time, showing the world the evidence of our high calling. The service remains the high point in my life, as did the ordination to the priesthood which took place 12 months later, The ordination service in the Prayer book contains the words, "Receive the Holy Spirit for the office and work of a Priest in the Church of God". How does one describe it? More than seven years had gone by since taking the first steps towards it, and now it was really happening and my life's work beginning. I can recall the details of the service and the face of the Bishop, Richard Parsons, as he shook hands afterwards, just as if it had happened only yesterday.

So now I was assistant curate at St Matthew's, New Kent Road in the Diocese of Southwark. The parish had arranged a welcome party for me but I never made it. Shortly after I arrived, in the middle of the midweek service in Church, I felt everything going round and round and had to be assisted outside into the fresh air. There was at that time a flu epidemic and the vicar put me in a taxi with directions to the driver to take me home to my parents in north London. On arrival there I found both of them also suffering with the flu, so I didn't tell them what I was doing there but pretended I had just come to see them. After a while I took my leave and went back to be unwell in my bed-sit in Trinity Square. I recovered in time of course, and began my curacy, All my memories of my time at St Matthew's are happy ones, and though it was a case of baptism by fire, it was a wonderful way to start out on the journey of my ministry.

In the many years since then I have kept in touch with some of the young people, and recently heard from an elderly man in Australia who wanted to know if the name of Ockwell he had come across in the newspaper could be linked to a young curate who had that name whom he had known before the war. Sure enough I am one and the same man. Another man rings me quite regularly, who was a small boy at the time and who is now living in Pinner and he keeps in touch with me by telephone. Recently I took part at Chichester Cathedral in a funeral service for Charles Pinder, a young man I had prepared for confirmation in 1938 and who went on to become Archdeacon of Lambeth.

The parish of St Matthew was teeming with life, with a good choir and organist and a band of faithful servers and also an excellent Scout and Guide group – the best I have known either before or since. They invited me to be at their summer camps and also to join in the production of a Gang Show. It was the custom then for Oxford and Cambridge University colleges and well-known public schools to support downtown parishes in London by setting up mission centres. Thus St Matthew's New Kent Road became St Matthew's Newington (that was the name of the deanery) and Cranleigh School Mission. From time to time the school choir would visit us and sing Evensong and occasionally the headmaster would preach the sermon. Likewise a party from the parish would visit the school and join in activities there.

Life was full of various happenings and on Fridays in Lent young people of the parish would attend the early morning Holy Communion service, and afterwards we would go to Jo Lyons Tea Shop just down the road and have breakfast together. Lyons Tea Shops have now disappeared but in those days they were commonplace and well known for their 'nippy' waitresses. Times change! Back then we had Liptons, ABC, Maple and Company, Home and Colonial Stores, Timothy Whites and Taylor's and several other shops with branches all over London, all of which have now disappeared.

The general standard of housing in parts of the parish came as a great a shock to me, even though I knew it was a difficult area. The tenement dwellings had no gardens, back or front, just concrete yards with a clothesline and a refuse bin, with rats scuttling to and fro across the path. On entering the doorway of the buildings, one found oneself in dark and gloomy surroundings with passageways going left and right. Front doors would appear in the gloom and there was no light except from a dirty fanlight two floors up, above the inside stairway. On each landing there was an old-fashioned yellow sink with a cold-water tap and a WC. This was the total toilet facility for the eight flats on each landing. There was a also a chute in which the residents were meant to put their rubbish, which then went down the chute into a large bin in the yard below. A good deal of the rubbish ended up on the stairs, which contributed to the awful smell.

'Livestock' was common to the rooms and to the occupants. Every time, before the arrival of a new tenant, a little green van came from the Borough Council and workmen fumigated the premises. I remember waking one night in my digs to find the bed alive with unwanted visitors, and because of this had to go and stay elsewhere while the Council workmen came and dealt with it.

I have to admit that at first I found it extremely hard going, and several times had to pray for courage before going to visit the old and the sick, but as time went by I came to know and care for the people and forgot their surroundings. The people were extremely kind and accepted their lowly station in life without any real grumbling or manifesting discontent. It was remarkable in the circumstances that many of them kept themselves very clean and well turned out. I remember Jack Bradley and Harry Brown (both of them later killed in the war), young Sunday School teachers who always turned up looking smart and clean.

The bad dwellings have long since been demolished, half by Hitler during the war and the rest by the Council afterwards. People, especially during the first years of the war, were always warm and considerate. "Come and sit down, dear, and I'll get you a cup of tea". There were times when the speaker would say, "I won't be a minute", and then disappear for a short time. In fact they had gone to the shop next door to buy a pennyworth of cow's milk for my tea, as they knew I did not care for the contents of the tin of condensed milk which always seemed to stand on the sheet of newspaper which served as a tablecloth.

Almost all children attended Sunday School so we had crowds of them to contend with each week. I inherited a squad of 23 Sunday School teachers and we met each Friday evening to prepare the lessons and programme for the following Sunday. Part of my job was to place special emphasis on work amongst children and young people, which included the Sunday School, youth club and the Scouts and Guides. I found little time on my hands, as in addition to Parish work and other activities I was invited each year to lecture at the Diocesan Summer School at Seaford (after the war this continued at Rottingdean in Sussex).

One morning I was on my way to the daily service in Church when a man stopped me and asked for some help. I passed this man each morning and wished him 'good day' but now I stopped and said, "How does it come about that I see you each morning going to work, and yet you are now asking me for help?" He replied, "No sir. You see me each morning going to look for work". He was a dock labourer, and the system then was that when a ship came in the dock gates were unlocked and the lucky ones got taken on. The rest went home and then came the next day to try again. No job, no pay. Fortunately things are different now.

On another day I was walking through the yard past a block of flats when a small child took my hand and walked with me. Nothing was said until I was about to leave, when she looked up at me and said, "Aren't you young!" I suppose I was - about 25 I think - and I imagine she thought every clergyman must be an old man. Similarly, a none-too-clean urchin came up to me one day and insisted I took one of his sticky sweets. I didn't want it, or need it, but loved having it. It made me think about our relationship with God. He doesn't need our prayers or worship but loves to have it so. It demonstrates a relationship and is altogether good.

As already mentioned, universities and public schools had Mission centres in the poorer parts of London, and not far from St Matthew's was Pembroke College Mission. The priest in charge was Frank Bishop - a very fine man. He came to see me and told me about East Street Market. The market is South London's equivalent of the huge market in East London's Petticoat Lane. Every Sunday morning the street is filled with stalls selling everything from the proverbial pin to a steamroller. Hundreds of people throng the area, and Frank said, "They don't come to us, so we ought to go to them".

His idea was that he, his curate, Charles McKenzie, and I should organise a miniature 'Hyde Park Corner' and go there each Sunday morning after our own Parish Communion service. So we planned to take a stand, and bought a soapbox. The idea was that the first member of the team of three would try and gather a crowd. The second would then ask the crowd to give him a couple of minutes or so while he talked about any subject he chose, topical or religious or both, and then the third man would get up and ask if there were any questions.

I agreed to have a go with the others, so off I went to East Street, after our church service on Sunday morning, to join the other two. You can imagine my feelings at the prospect, aged 25 and with no experience of speaking to hordes of people, most of whom could not care less about God or the church, and surely they would be far too busy to listen. But 'God moves in mysterious ways his wonders to perform', and although we did not know it, a certain well-known local Communist leader was used to gather a crowd for us.

No sooner had we 'set up shop' and one of us stood on the box than Mr Searson, for that was his name, began to heckle. We discovered that if someone heckles, nothing works better at gathering a crowd. People stop to find out what is going on, and then other people, seeing the crowd, stop to find out the reason for it. As soon as the crowd was big enough, the second man in our team got up and said, "Give me a couple of minutes or so, there is something I would like to say". The strange thing is that almost invariably the crowd listened, which gave the opportunity for one of us to talk and give some teaching from the

Outdoor preaching 1928-9

Christian point of view. After that, the third member got up and asked if there were any questions. More heckling then began, and many questions were asked.

One Sunday morning Mr Searson shouted out, "It's all poppycock. Jesus never even existed. There is nothing about it at all in the Encyclopaedia Britannica – nothing in it about Jesus or the Christian faith." Ordinary mortals do not own the Encyclopaedia Britannica – copies can be found in large public libraries - but it so happened that Frank Bishop did have the Encyclopaedia Britannica at home, and off he sped to fetch the copy where the right references could be found. On his return he got onto the box and said, "As I was coming back, a small boy stopped me and said, 'Watcher Father. Got yer telephone directory with yer?' 'No,' I said, 'I haven't. But the fact is you will find in the Encyclopaedia Britannica that there is page after page on the Christian faith, and the small boy reminded me to say that when you get home, pick up your telephone directory, look up the letter S, and you will find page after page giving the telephone numbers of Saint so-and-so school, hospital, care home and various other welfare organisations, all institutions springing from the Christian faith. Then look up the letter A and tell me how many organisations can be found under the word atheist. There is not one. All atheists have ever done is nothing but talk."

So every Sunday until the war came we went to East Street market, and I got quite used to talking in the open air and speaking 'off the cuff'. I discovered that when answering awkward questions one could play for time, and give oneself the opportunity to think, first by complimenting the speaker telling him or her what an important question had been asked, then repeating the question and saying, "If you'll give me a few moments of your time I'll do my best to answer". During this time one would be busy thinking of something to say and how to tackle the question. Many times I recalled sitting in at lectures in college and wondering what I was doing listening to all this, never imagining that years later I would find myself in East Street market recalling subjects I studied and thought I would never use.

My years at St Matthews left me with happy memories and made a splendid start to my career. Life was full in all sorts of ways, and I produced a revue called Matthewdeville which ran for several days and was repeated the following year. Much of the material I used came from plays and drama performed in my student days. At Christmas time we had the usual nativity play performed by children, and also one performed by older members of the congregation, and there was also a Passion play in Holy Week.

Life indeed was full and all kinds of things took place with parish socials, a fancy dress ball, and on every bank holiday a parish ramble. We would walk to Waterloo or London Bridge station, catch a train to the country and spend a happy day there. Many people loved these occasions.

The year 1938, however, saw clouds gathering on the international horizon and the rise of Hitler and Nazism. As

Matthewdeville

is well known, the Prime Minister at the time, Mr Chamberlain, went to see Hitler in Munich and came back with a piece of paper in his hand saying, "It is peace in our time". He was rather despised at the time for being too weak to stand up to Hitler and his string of broken promises and the invasion of other countries, but there is another school of thought which suggests that Mr Chamberlain's actions gave us another 12 months to prepare for the war which seemed more and more certain. England had made little preparation for war. The very idea of another war between Germany and ourselves seemed almost an impossibility. After the terrible slaughter of 1914/18 it was surely not possible that war would be declared again only 20 years later.

Hitler rose to power and eventually took the majority of his countrymen along with him. It has to be remembered that Germany had lost all its colonies and at the time there were millions of unemployed, and Germans felt that the dignity of their great nation had been destroyed. There were wonderful rallies, marching and uniforms, and Hitler took hold of the young people with his youth organisations. These massive rallies and all the other happenings at that time, together with the fact that he increased the army, navy and air force and extended German boundaries, caused very few to question their leader's policies. If people did so, they began to forget, or chose to ignore, what was happening in terms of anti-Semitism and concentration camps. Actually there were many anti-Nazis who gave their lives because they were not in favour of Hitler's policies.

Besides my duties at St Matthews, I carried on taking my turn in East Street, lectured at the summer school and took my first Three Hours service on a Good Friday at a local parish church. More and more signs of preparation for war became apparent, and though nobody dared think about it, war seemed to become ever more likely. Gas masks were distributed to everyone, and I took part in this task in the local school.

In August 1939, I went on holiday to stay with my sister Rosa, who lived at Saltash in Cornwall, just across the River Tamar. Her house was called 'Harbour View', and from her sitting room window there was a marvellous view of the harbour of Devonport and Plymouth. It so happened I was sitting looking out of the window and became aware that ship after ship of the Royal Navy was coming into port. I turned to my sister and said, "There's going to be a war. I must get back to my parish in London as soon as possible." So off I went the next day, September 1st, and that same day Hitler invaded Poland. Britain issued an ultimatum to Germany, saying, "Withdraw your forces by 11.00 am on Sunday, September 3rd, or we will declare war." Mr Chamberlain broadcast to the nation at 11.00 am on September 3rd and said that no response had been received from Hitler, and therefore we, Britain, were at war with Germany.

What we had hoped and prayed would not happen, did, and our emotions were a strange mixture of relief at the end of months of tension, and horror at what the future held. We expected immediate aerial bombardment and even poison gas, but this did not happen and air raids by German aircraft did not begin in earnest until the following spring.

The day war was declared was a Sunday and our main service was at 9.30. The entire congregation gathered in the hall afterwards to hear the broadcast by the Prime Minister on the BBC. When the awful truth set in, the older generation went quietly and sadly home, leaving the young people feeling excited and almost playful in their parody of being soldiers and serving in the defence of Britain. Several of these same young men would later give their lives for their country. I vividly remember the day when all the school children were evacuated to Devon, and recall the difficulty I had in holding back the tears as I stood by the church railings and watched the lines of children going to the station. Several of the children wrote to me from their new homes, but many of them drifted back to London when after several weeks no aerial bombardment had taken place.

There was a 'by-election' taking place in that part of London in the autumn. I can't remember why the by-election was being held, but Mr Searson, our chief heckler in East Street, was standing as a 'Stop the War' candidate. To me this brought home the difference between a democracy and a dictatorship. Here we were within sight and sound of Big Ben, in the centre of the capital city, engaged in a war, and this man was allowed to stand on a street corner and attack the Government and his country, claiming the war was a Capitalist affair and only Jewish financiers would profit from it. Not only did he shout about it, but the police were there just to keep order in case things got nasty and they also allowed him to put spurious leaflets through everybody's front door. What did we do about it? Nothing! Just imagine someone in Nazi Germany, in Berlin, speaking out against Hitler and not only allowed to be doing so but being protected by the German police!

The first months of the war were mostly free of air raids inland, though much activity took place at sea. The great and wonderful work undertaken by the air force, the navy and the merchant seamen in the war years was something never to be forgotten. In May 1940, Germany invaded the Low Countries and nearly swept all before them, and very nearly swept the British and French armies into the sea. The miracle of Dunkirk took place but we were now left just about defenceless, apart from the magnificent work of the men in the Royal Air Force who excelled themselves in the Battle of Britain, and prevented an almost certain invasion of our country.

At the Elephant and Castle life went on almost as usual until mid summer when there was a massive raid on London's docks and the surrounding area. Then began nightly visits of the German bombers. Air raid sirens sounded each evening at about 7, and people took to the shelters or went down to the underground stations. There are many stories of the heroism of the fire fighters and air raid wardens and the bravery of ordinary folk in the face of death and destruction. One incident in particular has always amused me and tells of the remarkable stoicism of the people. Lord Lichfield was having tea when a daylight raid took place and a bomb struck nearby. There was a loud explosion and bits of the ceiling fell down. "What was that, Nanny?' asked this small boy. The reply, "A bomb dear. Take your elbows off the table."!

During the blitz, the vicar and I would visit shelters every night and give what comfort we could. Because we were up most of the night, we normally rested in the afternoon, but one day I was making my way rather wearily back to my digs when I remembered I had promised to visit Mr and Mrs Grey and their children who lived in the top flat of one of the dwellings. I decided I was too tired to go back and see them, but then thought to myself I had promised and therefore I must go, so I turned back and climbed the stairs to their flat. While I was there we had a daylight raid, which was unusual – the bombing normally started around 7 pm and we could almost set our watches by the timing of it. Because of that daylight raid, I asked the family what they did at night. They said they didn't like the shelters so stayed where they were. I said I thought this was extremely unwise, and if they didn't like the shelters, why didn't they ask someone such as Mrs Robinson, who lived in a flat on the ground floor, if they could take shelter there every night?

I went home and returned in the evening for my usual tour of the shelters. That same night a man was taken ill in one of them, so I left and went across the yard to ask Mrs Robinson for some water. I knocked on the door, and when the door was opened I could see several people on the floor wrapped in blankets. Mrs Grey's voice piped up, "You see we have taken your advice." At that moment there was a terrific explosion and the building came down on top of us all. We had suffered a direct hit from a German bomb. There was pitch darkness and the sound of falling masonry but not one of us was badly injured, though I did have a large dent in the steel helmet I was wearing, and scratches on my legs and face. When an air raid warden shone a torch through the wreckage, and I could see light and hear a voice asking if there was anyone there, it was a wonderful moment.

Soon we were dug out and I was taken to Lambeth Hospital. One remarkable thing was that when my clothes were removed my body was covered in dust. The force of the explosion had penetrated dust right through the layers of clothing. On admission I was asked for the name and address of my next of kin – normal procedure, but I was very reluctant to give it because I did not want my elderly parents to be caused any worry. All to no avail. A policeman called at their bungalow at Peacehaven, near Brighton, and informed them I had been admitted to

I was 'inside' here when this was demolished on the 9th September 1940

Lambeth Hospital as an air raid casualty. They then set off on what was for them a long and difficult journey to the hospital. Naturally I was delighted to see them and grateful for their thought in making the journey and finding overnight accommodation in London. I raised the question of why my request that they should not be informed had not been granted, and they explained that, by law, next of kin must be told because if a person should die and no previous information had been given, there would be quite a few repercussions.

After my stay in hospital, the daily air raids

continuing, I returned to duty. The vicar informed me that due to the bombing there was not sufficient work any more for both us and he had volunteered as an Army chaplain. This meant he would go and I would stay. A few days later he told me the Army authorities had rejected him as too old (he was 50 I think) so he would stay and I was free to go. So that was how I became an Army chaplain.

Chaplain to the Forces

Several days after sending off an application to join the Army there was a loud knocking at the door, at 11 o'clock at night, and standing there was a policeman, who, after establishing my identity, informed me I must report at once to the headquarters of Eastern Command in Hounslow. I thought I must surely be urgently required, if it was important enough to send a policeman at night, but events were to prove otherwise and life followed at a very leisurely pace.

Next morning I set off for Eastern Command, and was there informed to acquire various items of uniform and make my way to Chester Teacher Training College. At Chester, with about 20 other potential Army chaplains, we had lectures and were told what we should do and should not do, and learned the difference between a brigadier and a grenadier. We also had a daily session of very strenuous physical training. Even now I can remember the stiffness in my joints!

When I left the City of Chester I vowed I would come back and see it again after the war. All of us potential padres were posted to different units, and I was instructed to join the 7th Battalion of the Oxford and Bucks Light Infantry and make my way to the headquarters of Southern Command at Salisbury. The easiest way to travel to Salisbury is to take a train to London and then change, but I was told I must take the shortest route, which is via Swindon. The railway system was all over the place because of the bombing, and I got to Swindon in the evening. Nothing for it but to stay the night and continue my journey next day. I had some cousins living in

Swindon, so presented myself on their doorstep and asked for a night's lodging, which of course was gladly given. In the morning I travelled to Salisbury and reported to the Officer Commanding Southern Command. He inspected my credentials and then said, "You are posted to the Oxford and Bucks Light Infantry and they are stationed in Devon, so take yourself to Devonport and report to the Officer Commanding there." He then looked at his watch and said, "You'll never get there today. Book a room and go tomorrow."

I did as I was told, and set off again the next day, and on arrival at Devonport I was met by a high-ranking officer, who said, "The Oxford and Bucks are stationed at Westward Ho, in North Devon." He then looked at his watch, and said, "You'll never get there today, so book a room and go tomorrow."

My sister, as mentioned, was living at Saltash, just across the river, so I travelled by train across the famous Brunel Bridge, and spent the night with my sister and her husband. Next day, Saturday, I made my way across the county of Devon to Bideford in the north, then up to a holiday camp at Westward Ho, which the army had requisitioned. On arrival, I reported to the adjutant of the Oxford and Bucks Light Infantry at the orderly room, and he said, "I suppose you have come to take a service tomorrow, Sunday." I replied that I thought this was one of the reasons I had come. Eventually he realised I was a permanent fixture, and sent for the quartermaster to fix me up with one of the holiday camp chalets, blankets etc. The journey to Westward Ho from Chester had taken four days, emphasising just how important I was to victory!

On Sunday I began my long association with the Oxford and Bucks, and did everything I could to get to know the men and serve them in every possible way. For instance if they went on a route march, so did I. If they went on a night exercise, I went with them.

One weekend stands out in my memory, because the Regimental Band of the Light Infantry came down and stayed with us and accompanied the parade service on Sunday, and we also marched with the band through the streets and villages of the surrounding district. The environs of Westward Ho were in marked contrast to the Elephant and Castle, and I thoroughly enjoyed it all and felt very conscious of my good fortune. Nearby was the village of Abbotsham, and the vicar called to see me at the holiday camp and invited me to preach at Evensong, which I did, and I preached at Abbotsham almost every Sunday evening while I was stationed there. He and his wife were very kind to me and I was able to enjoy the luxury of a bath and other facilities that were not of the highest order in the former holiday camp. I kept in touch with the Challenor family for many years until they died.

We had units of our regiment based at Bideford, Northam and Bude and our headquarters at Westward Ho. I travelled between them taking services whenever there was an opportunity. My time in Devon was altogether too short – just three months – and then we were off to Lyminge in Kent, not far from Folkestone, and right below air battles between the Germans and the Royal Air Force. The morning after we arrived, I set off with my batman/driver to explore the neighbourhood and had not gone very far when an enemy plane was shot down in a field close by. We scrambled over the hedge to give what help we could and made arrangements to get the pilot taken to hospital. Now, I thought, we really are caught up in action, but in the next five years I never saw another plane shot down.

As in Devon, units of the battalion were based in various places as a defence against possible invasion, and as before I visited them, took services, and sought to help in any way I could. I possess a record of every service I took during my Army career, and here I took services at Lyminge, Postling and Elham, and on Saturday April 5th 1941 presented 20 men for confirmation by the Bishop of Dover at St Mary's Church, Lyminge. During all my time in the Army I organised confirmation classes, and presented candidates at Lyminge and Canterbury Cathedral (both taken by the Bishop of Dover) at the Garrison Church, Colchester by the Bishop of Colchester, and at St Paul's Church, Clacton by the Bishop of Chelmsford. Also, later on, in Capetown Cathedral by the Archbishop of Capetown, then in the compound of the Iraq Petroleum Company in Kirkuk, Iraq, by the Bishop of Iran. Also by the Bishop of Lichfield at Caserta in Italy, and finally at Christ Church, Naples, by the Archbishop of York.

From Lyminge we moved to Whittersham and Appledore, still in the county of Kent, and as before had units in various parts of the area. This gave me plenty of opportunity for travel, and I went round arranging services in all kinds of places, including, always, the local parish church.

While we were in this particular area, General Montgomery became Divisional Commander and issued orders that all ranks were to undertake strenuous exercises in full battle order. These directions were not generally very welcome, and many were inclined to think he was somewhat 'off his rocker', especially when he gave orders that all officers were to attend a special meeting in a cinema in Folkestone. At that time, Folkestone was under continual bombardment from guns across the Channel, as well as aerial attack from the German Air Force. It would have been possible for a bomb or shell to have inflicted heavy casualties on the high ranking officers of the 56th London division all in one go. "How stupid", one would say, but it was quite deliberate and meant to impress in the minds of everyone that we were unafraid of the might of Germany and in no mood for giving up, even while things were very difficult and we were short of men and machines. The same show of spirit was manifested at various times later in the war, most notably, of course, at El Alamein.

People had, and still have, different views on General Montgomery, but in my mind there is no doubt that he was able to inspire the soldiers and spread an unconquerable spirit, while still showing he cared about the men under his command. Two years later, after the victory in North Africa, he came and inspected our regiment, and as soon as he arrived came directly to me and said, "We have met before." I agreed that we had, and he went on to question whether the men were getting their mail, and whether their general welfare was up to scratch.

After our stay at Whittersham and Appledore, which lasted six months, we moved to the military barracks at Colchester, and services were held in the garrison church. While I was stationed there I travelled to various wartime aerodromes such as Great Stanford, Castle Kent and Homington, as well as taking services at various parish churches in the neighbourhood. One parish church in particular stands out in my memory, and this is St Mary, Dedham, a famous church because it is associated with the artist John Constable. When I was in the Scouts, aged about 14, we camped nearby one Easter, and attended the parish church on the Easter Sunday morning. I little dreamed then that one day I would be standing at the altar, taking the service, and preaching from the pulpit. While stationed at Colchester there was an interregnum at Dedham, so I took several services there and loved doing it.

After our stay in the barracks at Colchester there came a very pleasant interlude at Clacton-on-Sea. Because all seaside places were prohibited areas with barbed wire and anti-tank obstacles all along the beaches, everywhere in the area was practically deserted, and I found it a very delightful experience. All the piers round the coast were cut in two, to prevent enemy forces landing on the pier and making their way inland. Clacton was no exception, but there was a rope ladder joining the two halves of the pier, and I made my way across it and entered the pier pavilion at the far end. This gave me a weird feeling, because the concert-party of August 1939 had obviously been told to pack up and go as soon as possible, and there in the theatre were various dusty props and stage directions, all left as if the show was just about to go on.

All good things come to an end, and after two months in Clacton we moved again. Our destination now was a campsite in a very remote part of the country near Woodbridge in Suffolk. 'Old soldiers' in the regiment said we were bound for service overseas, as the powers that be always move you to some outlandish place you will be glad to see the back of, before sending you on embarkation leave. Sure enough, after a couple of months we were given two weeks' embarkation leave. Every Division in the Army had its own logo, and in our Division (the 56th London Division), all of us had on our shoulders scarlet patches with a black cat – Dick Whittington's cat - printed on it, so although our movements were supposed to be 'hush-hush', the mainline stations in London were flooded with hundreds of soldiers, all displaying the black cat on each shoulder. It would not have taken an enemy agent very long to put two and two together and find out about our movements.

Over the sea and far away

Embarkation leave came to an end, and at the stations in London were tearful wives and sweethearts saying farewell to their loved ones. We entrained to the River Clyde in Scotland, and on arrival boarded a troopship. We had no idea where we were going but guessed it was somewhere east, as all our vehicles were now painted sand colour. The ship stayed in port for about a week, while other ships were organised and a convoy made up ready to sail. The convoy system is a way of protecting ships from attacks by submarines. It means that a group of ships move together, ringed round by destroyers, and in the centre of the ring there are larger naval vessels.

The day came when we were on the move, and the soldiers, when we left, were singing songs such as "There'll always be an England" and "We'll meet again some sunny day, don't know where, don't know when, but I know we'll meet again some sunny day". But as the land became more and more indistinct, silence fell and one could tell the thoughts of everyone on leaving England, homes and families. Some were newly married, some with wives expecting babies, and all very full up, knowing that some would never see their loved ones again. But just then a destroyer sped past our ship, and as it went by a voice came over the loudhailer, "Coo, what a lovely looking lot of soldiers". Whether it was done intentionally or not we shall never know, but it caused a burst of laughter, relieved the tension, and everyone settled down to their future life on board the troopship.

Our ship was a former passenger liner, the SS Almanzora. I do not know how many passengers and crew she was meant to carry, but on board when we sailed were nearly 3,000 men, a brigade of three battalions each of around 1000. We were more than a little crowded! Down on the lower decks, everything had been cleared and long bench-like tables installed for the men. They actually slept in hammocks and fed and relaxed at the same benches. The submarine menace was at its height at the time, and we were ordered to wear life jackets round the clock. Britain was currently losing ships at a rate faster than they could be replaced and as we sailed, every ten minutes a hooter would sound from the Commodore's ship and we all changed course. This left no time for a U-boat commander to get us in focus and fire a torpedo, so we zig-zagged across the ocean and our journey was very much longer than it would have been if we had not been dodging U-boats the whole way.

Looking back it was obvious that if our ship had been attacked, most of the men on board would not have stood an earthly chance of survival. I don't recall any feeling that we were in great danger, and I suppose it was the same for me as in the blitz, which I didn't mind at all at the start of the air raids, but after being hit, any time a bomb landed anywhere near I found myself automatically cringing, wondering if it was going to come anywhere near me.

On our first morning after departure we awoke to find ourselves out of sight of land, but with an amazing sight of all these merchant ships moving together, surrounded by a ring of destroyers with larger naval vessels in the centre of the ring. Our ship was to be home to us for two months and we had to make the best of it. As a child I had been fond of playing Lotto, which for some reason on board ship was known as "Housey Housey". Today it is known as Bingo and this and other games were played. I held daily confirmation classes and also organised entertainments and variety shows, which called forth extraordinary talents from some of the men. Over the weeks of the voyage the shows were called "Freetown Frolics", "Capetown Capers", Mombassa Madness" and "Bombay Bombast". Every day a church service was held in a suitable part of the ship, and on Sunday morning in the first class lounge, and my register records that over 400 men were packed in together.

When the first variety show was ready, I asked the OC Troops (Officer Commanding Troops) for permission to use the first class lounge for its production. This was refused and we had to stage the show squeezed in between the rows of benches on the lower decks. How we managed it I don't know, but we did. My relationship with the OC Troops was rather poor, and even poorer after this happened! Because there were three battalions on board, each with a commanding officer, it was thought necessary to have a senior officer responsible for all the troops on board the ship – the OC Troops. Ours was a former retired colonel, and at the first Sunday morning service I was aware of the colonel sitting in the front row, fiddling about and not paying much attention to what was going on.

Sometime after the service finished I went back to my cabin and found a note addressed to me 'From OC Troops, Subject: Divine Service', and saying that if the service was to be held in future, it must not be longer than 30 minutes. I cannot remember how long it had actually lasted, but I was not used to being told how long a service should take and did not intend to be told at that time. So off I went to his cabin, went in and said, "You wished to see me." He got up and said that he had not sent for me, so I showed him the memo he had left for me. "Oh yes, old boy," he said. "You can't hold the attention of the men any longer than that, so 30 minutes is the limit". I didn't take very kindly to this instruction, and didn't take much notice!

Because of this episode, and the fact that I had expressed my great displeasure when he refused to let the men use the first class lounge for the production of our variety shows, he reported me to the ship's Captain! By this time I had become good friends with the Captain and the First Officer, so when the Captain asked me to come to his cabin he just smiled at me and said, "Forget it, padre".

After more than two weeks on board we arrived at Freetown, Sierra Leone. The harbour there was shelter to a number of large naval ships, and somehow I felt encouraged by the sight of them all. We then sailed on to Cape Town, and the captain told me that for purposes of refuelling, the convoy was splitting into two halves, and our half would have to go to Durban as we hadn't got enough fuel to take us all the way from Cape Town to our next port of call. In fact we found ourselves in the half of the convoy heading for Cape Town and the other half went on to Durban! I shall never forget being awakened by my friend Patrick Montgomery, calling out, "Padre! Padre! Come and see the most marvellous view of Capetown and the Table Mountain in the early morning sunshine".

We docked after four weeks at sea and were greeted by groups of people offering to take parties for sightseeing. It was a wonderful welcome, and I was linked to a family who drove me round for the five days we were there and treated me right royally. It was all very delightful, and made all the more so for me because I had been able to arrange a special confirmation service in Cape Town Cathedral taken by the Archbishop of Cape Town, and presented men I had prepared for confirmation on board ship. The environment and the scenery were altogether lovely and never to be forgotten.

All good things come to an end, and off we sailed. Our ship did not call into Durban as the captain had told me it should have done, and so half way across the Indian Ocean we left the main convoy and, accompanied by a cruiser, made our way to Mombasa. Two things stand out about our time there. One was the change from day to night with a complete absence of twilight. We were so near to the equator it was almost as if someone had simply switched off the light. The second thing was that I was taken to a dentist for treatment, as during the voyage I had broken a piece off a tooth! Our short stay there gave us a glimpse of the tropics and was very fascinating.

Now we were bound for Bombay and India. In my mind's eye I can still see the morning we arrived – India, recognisable to me from the pictures I had seen quite often of the Gateway to India at the entrance to Bombay Harbour. We stayed several days and took every opportunity for sightseeing, and while I was there I managed to make contact with a former fellow student based in Bombay and was able to go and see him.

We were not meant to stay long in India – only to wait until a smaller ship became available to transport us to Basra at the head of the Persian Gulf. In due course we went on board the SS Santria. The heat of that journey remains with me vividly, and as many of the men as possible slept on the deck to try and avoid the stifling conditions down below. When we arrived in Basra we were under canvas, and made ourselves as comfortable as possible in the sand and heat. One week later we started out by train for Baghdad. The train journey was so uncomfortable it seemed as if the carriages had square wheels! I was dozing in the corner of one of the carriages, by the window, when the train stopped and I looked up and saw the title of the station. It had only two letters, U R – Ur, and I realised that this was Ur of the Chaldees in ancient Mesopotamia and the birthplace of Abraham. I jumped out of the train, and just as quickly jumped back in again, just so that I could say that I had placed my foot in Abraham's birthplace.

It seemed extraordinary when we reached Baghdad that we had to leave the train and march across the city to take another train to Kirkuk in the north of the country. It seemed extraordinary at the time, but then I realised exactly the same sort of thing would happen in London. If one arrives at Waterloo, Victoria or Charing Cross and want to go north one must cross London to King's Cross or St Pancras and then take another train. Anyway, after four months we arrived at Kirkuk, which had nothing to recommend it at all, and we settled down in what seemed much like a cement yard – just miles of white sand, and again we were under canvas. The locals, we discovered, if not anti-British were certainly pro-German, and swastikas were marked in the sand which were signs of the possible

Camp in Iraq

arrival of the German air force. There was, of course, no church, or anything like it, as a centre for worship, so in the camp I was given a marquee and set out to furnish it with the aid of petrol cans and anything else I could lay my hands on.

It was getting near Christmas, and all of us were feeling a bit homesick with no news of any sort from home. When at last mail did arrive, the noise around the camp was deafening. We were ordered to dig down inside our tents so that we slept below ground level, and at nightfall petrol cans were filled with sand and petrol and set alight to illuminate the whole campsite. The reason for this was that the local Kurds were apt to raid the campsite and take pot shots at the tents, hence the requirement to dig down so that we slept with our heads below ground level to avoid any stray bullets.

What were we doing in Kirkuk? In theory we were guarding the oilfields from invasion, or possible invasion, by the German army coming in from the North. At that time they were making great progress towards the Caucasus Mountains. We were designated PAI force – short for Persia and Iraq force – and on paper quite a formidable army. However, I was ordered to attend a conference of Chaplains in Baghdad, and the notice I received was addressed to the Padre of a long list of units. When we assembled I discovered our numbers were really quite small, and I realised that most of the units existed only on paper. This was supposed to hoodwink the Germans into thinking the British Army was much stronger than it actually was. Both sides practised this sort of game. Legend has it that the Germans built an airport in France, constructed entirely from wood, including wooden airplanes and so on. When it was finished, the

RAF went over and dropped wooden bombs on it! It was a game that both sides were playing, but it showed that even in war one needs a sense of humour.

In Iraq we were playing exactly the same sort of game, pretending we were much stronger than we were. Iraq, then and now, is the centre of the oil industry, and at that time it was even more important than it is today because we had no oil supply other than that which came from the Middle East. The Iraq Petroleum Company, or IPC, is a British owned company and still has a large settlement there. Employees from England had a clubroom

With IPC workers in Iraq

and concert hall, with gardens irrigated and displaying roses and other lovely flowers, reminding everybody of home. Everything was very well kept, and in marked contrast to the surrounding desert. The oil pipeline from Kirkuk crosses the land to the port of Haifa and from there the oil is transported by tanker to England or wherever. The pipeline had to be guarded because it was always being subjected to attack – often successfully.

One of the officers in the Oxford and Bucks regiment had some friends working at IPC, so he got in touch with them. Through him I was introduced to them and was able to visit their well kept and lovely house, and I was offered the opportunity to take a bath and enjoy various other facilities not normally found in an Army camp in northern Iraq! I was also able to contact the Church of England Bishop in Iran and arrange a confirmation service in the concert hall at IPC (the bishop normally visits IPC every now and again as part of his ministry in Persia and Iraq). Apart from the confirmation, which took place in March 1943, my normal routine order of church services was held in the church tent, which was my headquarters. Services at 6.30 and 11.30 pm were held on Christmas Eve, and also at 6.15, 7.15, 8.00, 9.00 10.00 11.00 and 12.00 on Christmas Day, and some of those were attended by over 500 men. Units of the Royal Fusiliers had joined our own regiment, and the whole encampment was spread over a large area. Hence many services were taken in different parts of the camp.

Just before Christmas, the Commanding Officer got me to travel north to the city of Mosul to get whatever supplies I could to make Christmas for the men rather more like home than it would otherwise have been. So off I went to bring back dates, nuts, fruit and anything else I thought helpful. On the return journey my driver and I passed through Erbil, thought to be one of the oldest cities in the world. We then discovered the ruins of Nineveh and I found all this very exciting because much of it is written about in the Old Testament. Nineveh especially takes up much of the Book of Jonah. At this time my vehicle was a PU, which is short for Public Utility. Having a public utility vehicle instead of a rather nice staff car was very much a bit of a come down, so I named the PU 'Ichabod', which in Hebrew means 'The Glory is Departed', and this word was painted for me on the bonnet of the vehicle.

'Ichabod' with batman/driver, Iraq 1942

The reason for our sojourn in Iraq was soon brought to an end, because against all the odds and as a result of tremendous resistance by the Russians, the Germans were defeated at the Battle of Stalingrad. So once again we were on the move after a stay of five months in that part of the world, and now began an exciting journey across the desert to northern Palestine, arriving just north of the Sea of Galilee.

Much of Iraq is very arid, and the joy of seeing and being in the Holy Land, with its wonderful carpets of flowers everywhere, was altogether inspiring. Given the opportunity we all scampered about picking wild flowers, and I still have some pressed flowers in my register from those days 64 years ago. In the New Testament Jesus talks about the fact that "even Solomon in all his glory was not arrayed like the lilies of the field." The lilies of the field are thought to be anemones, which grow wild in that part of the land and carpet the hillsides with colour in the spring. On and on we went down through Israel and the Sinai desert, and in April 1943 reached Tel Akabar in Egypt and then had a long, long trek to join the 8th Army through El Alamein, Tobruk, Bengazi and Tripoli to Enfidaville on the borders of Tunisia.

One day, on my way up to the front line to join Major Pat Montgomery and "B" Company, a hail of German shells landed around me. I threw myself onto the ground and hoped for the best. When this particular bombardment was over I continued up to the front and was greeted by Pat with, "Gosh Padre! Were you out there?" I was unhurt but very frightened. In such circumstances it is natural to pray, "God help me and keep me safe", and I certainly prayed more than a little, several times. The experience made me think about the substance of my prayers. Why should God keep me safe? What about the men alongside me, all of them somebody's husband, sweetheart, son or best friend? I decided the right form of prayer should be something similar to: 1. Oh God if I am to die let me come into your presence. 2. If I am wounded help me to bear it with courage and as an example to others, and 3. If I am allowed to live, help me to be more devoted and true to my high calling. I have lived to tell the tale and hopefully I have made worthwhile use of my many years.

The German army in North Africa surrendered at the end of April 1943 and I have vivid pictures in my mind of thousands of German troops walking towards us to become prisoners of war.

One of the tasks of an Army padre in wartime is that

of burying the dead - not exactly a pleasant job but it must be done. Before burial takes place, personal papers have to be removed and later on sent back to Headquarters, together with a map reference of where the burial took place, so that the body can be exhumed and reburied in a military cemetery. One burial in particular stands out for me and that was of a German soldier. As usual I removed his personal papers and his wallet, but inside the wallet was a photograph of a charming young German woman with two lovely little children. Written across the photo was "All my love forever, darling." Somehow this brought home to me very forcibly the horror of war and the fact that war means we are killing and wounding each other. When will we ever learn? I can see that photograph very clearly in my mind's eye, even after 65 years. "When comes the promised time that war shall be no more, when lust, oppression, crime shall flee Thy face before?" As I write we are at war in Iraq and Afghanistan, and there is trouble in the Holy Land, Abyssinia and other parts of the world.

The war in North Africa had ended and our regiment moved back to Tripoli. Among other happenings we had an inspection by General Montgomery, and he recalled the fact we had met before in south east England, and enquired if the men were getting their mail and everything necessary for their welfare. He called a meeting of all the officers of the 8th Army in a large theatre in Tripoli and began his address by saying, "There will be an interval of five minutes during which you may cough, after which there will be no coughing."! He went on to say that we were not sitting on the shores of the Mediterranean for a holiday, but had to prepare for the all-important and tremendous step of gaining a foothold again in Europe, and we were preparing to invade Sicily and Italy.

Part of our training consisted of boarding a troop landing craft and practising landings on the African coast. We jumped off the ship into the sea right up to our armpits, and got to land soaking wet. This did not matter that much because the sun soon dried us out. We were told landing craft would come in close to the land in the real invasion - they didn't! All training started at 4am before the intense heat of the day. The contrast in temperature was often dramatic. Sweaters and greatcoats first thing in the morning and then gradually disrobing as the sun came up. At Christmas time in Iraq we could sit outside sunning ourselves, but at night it became bitterly cold and I used a tremendous amount of bedclothes endeavouring to keep warm.

In our free time, after our official duties were over, we were able to explore the neighbourhood, and several times I visited Sabrata, a lovely ancient Roman port with exciting ruins alongside the clear blue sea, providing us with excellent sea bathing. Returning to England after the war I could not get used to the cold grey sea round our coast and was forever comparing it adversely with the blue waters of the Mediterranean Sea.

Because of Allied air raids, the harbour at Tripoli (our headquarters) was crammed with shipwrecks, which served as a reminder of the major part played by the navy and the air force in supplying our needs. If one stops to think about it and is aware of the essential supplies required by an army of many thousands on the move, one realises the important part played by the back-up forces.

Victory in North Africa was a welcome and outstanding event. During the first years of the war Britain had little to celebrate, but now King George V came out to inspect and congratulate his victorious army.

The day before he came, our troops were formed up and lined the route. A General riding in an open-top car (as a stand-in for the king) swept by. The drill was repeated next day when the King did pass by. The whole exercise was intended as an acknowledgement of the great efforts and sacrifice of the Army, Navy and Air Force in achieving victory against the German forces, but it caused us to stand to attention in the very great heat and give His Majesty an 'artificial' Three Cheers.

Three days before his arrival we had biscuits and no bread. He was expected to visit the army bakery, and the bakery must be spotless, not baking bread! The result was that the visit, instead of bringing pleasure to the troops, succeeded in rubbing them up the wrong way! Given the chance, they would have cheered the King to the echo. Is it really necessary for royal visits to be prepared for and rehearsed in this way? Not much changes it seems, because in recent years the Queen Mother was due to visit and have tea at a certain theological college. Everything had to be acted out the day before, even to the extent of having a tea party with a stand-in Queen Mother.

Italy had surrendered in the spring of 1943, and the time for our invasion of Europe grew steadily nearer. At this point life for me took an unexpected turn. I was suddenly smitten with a raging fever and rushed to Tripoli hospital. I don't remember much about it, but remained there for more than a fortnight before being sent to a hotel for convalescence. Soon, I thought, I would be able to get back to my unit, but after 10 days the fever returned and I was readmitted to hospital. After another 10 days I was placed on a hospital ship and sailed down to Port Said in Egypt. On arrival there I was moved to a hospital at El Balla, right next to the Suez Canal - so close it seemed it would be possible to lean out of the window and touch the ships as they sailed by.

Another three weeks in that hospital and I was offered convalescence either in Alexandria, Cairo or Jerusalem and could make my own choice. Of course I chose Jerusalem, and went by train to Lady MacMichael's Convalescence Home, situated not far from the King David Hotel in Jerusalem. As I recovered I was able to wander around the old city and see all the Biblical sites with no tourists anywhere and no pressure on time. All very wonderful, and a great bonus after being so unwell. Two weeks went swiftly by, and I was then told to entrain for Cairo and arrived there on All Saints Day, November 1st 1943. I was handed a bundle of letters, one of which contained news that my father had died unexpectedly three weeks before. I applied for compassionate leave to go and see my mother but this was not granted.

Next day, my first in Cairo, was November 2nd, All Souls Day and I was able to take a Requiem for my father in the lovely Anglican Church of All Saints, and subsequently I took several services there. My stay in Cairo lasted four weeks during which time I took services at the Citadel and at various other Army centres. The Citadel was built by Saladin in 1166 and has remarkable domes and towers. Inside it is rather like a city within a city. I enjoyed exploring the ancient city of Cairo, and towards the end of my stay I was made aware of some extraordinary security arrangements. It didn't take much to realise that something very special was about to happen. Someone had whispered in my ear, "If you go to the cathedral about 5pm you might see something to your advantage." Naturally I went along and sat at the back and watched the entry of the leaders of the Allies accompanied by their chiefs of staff, with military police protecting them. They were coming in for a special service before a meeting to be held in Cairo, and then they would go on to meet Stalin in Tehran. So on the 23rd November 1943 I saw Winston Churchill, General Chang Kai Chek, President Roosevelt, Admiral Mountbatten and other VIPs.

Being unwell way back in August gave me some wonderful extra experiences and opportunities for extended travel, certainly not planned or expected. After a month in Cairo I was informed I must go to Alexandria and board a ship to take me to Italy and rejoin my unit. I took myself to the third of the three centres I had been offered as places for convalescence - Jerusalem, Cairo and Alexandria - an amazing opportunity resulting in fascinating experiences. At Alexandria I boarded a ship which had on board the 5th Indian Division, reinforcements for the battle which was going on in Italy. This Indian division had a very high reputation for bravery and professionalism, and I found quite a few of them were Christians who attended the service which I held on board each morning at 7 a.m. We sailed down the Mediterranean to the Port of Taranto in the south of Italy.

Four days after arrival in Italy I was in Naples and took the Sunday Services in the British and American Church of Christ Church. From there I made my way to the River Garigliano where the British Army was dug in on the south bank of the river, and at last I rejoined the 7th Battalion of the Oxford and Bucks Light Infantry, just six days short of four months after I had been taken ill. By now it was nearly Christmas and church services on Christmas Eve and Christmas Day took place with a background noise of gunfire. No Christmas truce as in the

First World War. In different parts of the line Carol Services were held, and there were two celebrations of Holy Communion on Christmas morning. In addition, both in the morning and in the afternoon, I held three Carol Services with different units who were spread over different parts of the front line. It was not an ideal situation, but I was glad to be back on duty with my Regiment once again, even though it meant I also had to take a number of funerals. It is difficult for most people to realise what it is like to have to take a burial service for friends and companions - not the happiest time in the life of an Army padre.

Unfortunately my return to active service proved to be of very short duration, because I was taken ill again and spent two weeks in a Military Hospital in Caserta and then ten days at the lovely resort of Sorrento. Surely the Sorrento peninsula is one of the most beautiful parts of Italy, and not only of Italy, but also of the world.

Hospital Chaplain

What of the future for me? I was no longer much use as a chaplain to an Infantry Regiment. I had been with the infantry all my time since I joined the Army in 1940, though I had only been with them for two weeks out of the previous six months. It was decided that I should be posted to a military hospital where I could receive treatment when necessary but also be of some service to the Army as a hospital chaplain. Accordingly I travelled to Nocera, a small village just south of Naples and north of Salerno, where I joined 103 General Hospital occupying a former Italian army barracks and with over 2,000 beds. I had no experience of life as a full-time chaplain, and wondered how the doctors and nurses would receive me. The hospital had large two-storey blocks either side of what had once been the parade ground. At the near end there was the administration block, and at the far end the NAAFI. NAAFI is short for Navy, Army and Air Force Institute, and is the place where recreational activities and canteen facilities take place. Most of the up-patients and staff, when not on duty, spend their spare time there and they can get refreshments and ordinary every day needs.

In the centre of the grounds was a large marquee, which I was informed was the Church Tent. If I had misgivings about how I would be received by the medical and nursing staff, these were soon dispelled because everyone could not have been more welcoming and anxious to assist me in my ministry. Every morning a service was held in the tent, and every day I was joined by some members of the staff. Visiting all the patients was a daily task but the sheer size of the hospital meant seeing each patient was only possible at intervals of several days, though emergencies and seriously ill patients were seen day or night. When conveys of wounded arrived it was a case of everyone with a pair of hands being called on to help, including of course the padre. One day one of the patients asked me if I got bored just going round the wards, and I said, "I don't suppose you realise how many beds there are in this hospital? In fact nearly 2,000, and that means if I spend just one minute with each patient it will take 2,000 minutes before I get round to see you again."

Ward services were held at regular intervals, and on my first Sunday in the Church tent they were held at 6.30, 7.30, 8.30 and 9.30am, plus12 noon and 6pm. These arrangements were made to meet the needs of the large staff and the many up patients. On Christmas Eve six services took place plus seven short epilogues in the wards, and on Christmas Day itself, another five services beginning at 6.30 a.m. Not much rest for the padre! Very soon I persuaded the senior medical officer to allow me to take over part of an unused section of the barracks for use as a chapel. Some beautiful furnishings made of Sorrento woodwork were supplied. (When I left the hospital 18 months later I asked for this furniture, because it was so lovely, to be shipped back to England and used in a suitable location. I was promised this would be done but nothing ever arrived.) We had a piano in the chapel for accompanying the services, played by Sergeant Jacky Mabbut, a medical orderly who was a wonderful pianist and also composer, and he formed and trained a staff choir. Outside the Chapel, a notice board made by the hospital carpenter proclaimed 'St Luke's Chapel' and gave the usual times of services.

Besides my work on the wards, I did my best to meet

the needs of the staff in every way possible and confirmation classes took place leading later on to a confirmation service taken by the Archbishop of York in Christ Church, Naples. We also produced a Passion Play, one I had used before during Holy Week at St Matthew's, New Kent Road in London, and this was produced not only at the hospital but also at the San Carlo opera house in Naples, thus making it available for a larger audience drawn from army units stationed around the area.

The hospital had the help of three chaplains, Church of England, Roman Catholic and Free Church. Sad to relate that at that time relations between denominations were at a low ebb. To our shame two incidents underlined this. As already mentioned, outside the chapel of St Luke there was a notice board, and the carpenter had made it in such a way that it formed a cross at the top. One morning, soon after it was erected, I went over to take the usual early service and found the cross had been broken off. I imagined someone had indulged in some vandalism the night before, after perhaps too much to drink. But later on in the morning the Free Church Chaplain came into my room, threw the cross onto my table and said, "My people have the cross in their hearts". I picked it up, stared at him and at the cross, and said, "My people, of course, have not". The cross on the notice board was replaced the same day.

Just before Christmas, one of the hospital sisters riding in a jeep - no seat belts in those days - was involved in an accident and thrown out of the vehicle. She hit her head on the kerb and subsequently died. She was a member of the C of E, so it was my job to organise and take the funeral service. Several of the nurses were Roman Catholics and naturally wished to attend the funeral. The

Roman Catholic chaplain forbade them to do so! Just imagine, they could eat together, work together, share sleeping accommodation together, but could not attend the funeral of one of their fellow nurses. Fortunately, nowadays such a thing certainly would not happen. Even if we are still dis-united, sharing in services and other such things is now commonplace.

Among the patients there were a number of Germans, and one officer I remember particularly because he never ceased proclaiming that Germany would win the war. We showed him maps and told him the Allies were overwhelming their forces and moving into Germany and soon the war would be over and end in our victory. Fritz, as we called him, informed us that Germany had a secret weapon and this would change everything. Back in England there was the advent of the V1 flying bomb and then the V2 rockets. After the war it became known that Germany had been developing an atomic bomb and had also built enormous underground factories where rockets were being mass-produced. Had the war lasted much longer, and the bomb and the profusion of rockets had landed on England, I tremble to think what would have happened. How our country which had stood up so wonderfully well in the blitz, and borne V1s and V2s, would have stood up to the atomic bomb and masses of rockets is beyond one's imagination. Until the very end, Fritz went on believing that Nazi Germany would win. He certainly knew more than we did at that time in early 1945.

Every evening while Chaplain of the hospital I went to the NAAFI and moved round chatting to the men and members of the staff, and each day there was present there an immaculately dressed Royal Military policeman. He was polite and well spoken and he informed us he worked in the hospital at night time because there had been reports of a series of thefts from patients' lockers, so he patrolled the wards after lights out. He was always there in the NAAFI every evening and everyone spoke well of him. Being on duty at night he said he had to sleep in the day, but one day the chief medical officer carried out an inspection of the staff sleeping quarters and saw this man in bed. "Why is that man in bed in the daytime?" he asked, and the quartermaster said, "It's the Royal Military Policeman who's here because of the thefts in the wards." "What thefts? What Royal Military Policeman?" In fact, this man, so well spoken, so well turned out, was Absent Without Leave and was the thief himself. He did his work in the night time, as he said, and therefore was not up and about in the day. In the end he landed up in jail, but I couldn't help thinking how clever these sort of people are, and what a pity it is they use their capabilities in the wrong way.

Not long after I arrived at the hospital I was awoken by someone banging on my door and calling out, "Sir, Sir, it's raining ashes!" I thought I must be dreaming, but the knocking continued and I got up and looked out of the window. Sure enough, it was raining ashes. What had happened was an eruption of the volcano Vesuvius, situated about five miles away. Ground shaking soon accompanied the raining of ashes and everything was plunged into darkness because of a cloud of ash blocking out the light of the sun. Vesuvius is notable because of the eruption that took place in AD78, when it erupted and destroyed the village of Pompeii and inhabitants of other villages nearby. Excavations have revealed the outline and foundations of many of the buildings of Pompeii and this place is now a great tourist attraction.

People were buried alive in and around the environs of Pompeii because of the eruption of Vesuvius in the first century, and because we knew this it was a more than frightening experience.

The deposit of ash got deeper and deeper, and patients from the wards upstairs were brought down to the ground floor because of the danger of the weight of ash breaking down the roof. Many cottages in the nearby villages suffered this fate. We had no idea how long the eruption would last, but in fact it began to ease off after about 48 hours. By then several inches of deposit were everywhere, and covered everything just like a heavy fall of snow. As soon as possible, the Army sent bulldozers and cleared the roads and pathways, and piles of clinker and ash could be seen all over the grounds and in the vicinity of the hospital.

Aftermath of Vesuvius eruption, 1944

Eighteen months later most of this was still there and one could see it for miles around. Maybe the Italians have got round to clearing it by now! In the normal course of events there were deaths at the hospital and funerals took place at the British military cemetery south of Salerno, 20 miles away. On my way there after the eruption I could see how the volcanic deposit got less and less until it finally petered out.

Every Wednesday afternoon I conducted an outing for up-patients to see the ruins of Pompeii, and because of it became very familiar with the interesting parts of the fine Roman town that had been there once upon a time. There are streets with pedestrian crossings, and marks of chariot wheels can be seen and there is a wonderful Amphitheatre. Today it is well known to many people because of holiday companies running tours to places like Pompeii, so many readers will have seen Pompeii for themselves. One Wednesday afternoon a small Italian girl attached herself to me, and after that, every Wednesday, she joined me at the gate and accompanied me on my way round. She gave me a small picture of Pompeii Church which I put in my wallet, and it is still there today, 64 years later.

Although it was wartime, Service people still got periods of 48 hours leave and I managed to do quite a lot of travelling. The road from Salerno to Sorrento is one of the most wonderful and breathtakingly beautiful roads in the world. We had a chaplains' conference at Amalfi and visited Ravello, situated in the hills above, and I also visited Positano, Capri and Sorrento. Memories of this

Positano on the Amalfi coast

lovely place stay with me, but after the war I began to think perhaps it really was not so beautiful as I imagined - perhaps I had romanticised about it. I was pleased to be proved wrong!

Many years later, a member of the congregation, a naval officer, at Westbourne in West Sussex where we were then living, was absent from church for about three years. One Sunday morning he reappeared and I asked him where he had been. It transpired he had come back to England after a spell as Naval Attaché in Naples. I told him I'd been in that part of the world during the war and always hoped that one day I would return, but I had never been back because I did not know where to stay and did not really know how to get back there. He said, "I've got the very place for you," and this turned out to be the Hotel Garden at Ravello. I got the full address from him, and then got in touch with Anna, the proprietor of the hotel, and fixed up a holiday for Muriel and myself.

Words fail me at the delight and joy of everything that followed. Ravello is stunningly attractive, and has the Villa Rufolo and the Villa Cimbrone, with incredibly wonderful

View of the Mediterranean coast from Villa Cimbrone, Ravello

views of the coastline of the Mediterranean. The Hotel Garden is built into the cliff-side and visitors go down to reception and down again to the bedrooms, and from every bedroom window is this glorious view. Anna's family run the hotel, her uncle is a waiter, and so on. We have been back several times, and now we are no longer able to travel members of our family continue to holiday there. This entire district on the coast of the Mediterranean from Salerno to Sorrento is delightful. When I was first there it was during the war, with no tourists and very little traffic, so I saw it all at its very best.

On another 48-hour leave from the hospital I went to see the glories of Rome and Assisi. Then in the autumn of 1944 we heard that a party of VAD Nurses was coming to join the staff at 103 General Hospital and one of these nurses was Muriel Hodgkinson who became my right hand lady when we were married in April 1946. Muriel was sometimes able to get leave at the same time as myself and joined me on expeditions to Capri and Ischia On the day the war ended I took her round the village in the jeep I had at my disposal, and what fun it all was! Six years of war, and now it was not easy to take in the fact that it really was all over, and our thoughts could turn to England and home.

On leave!

Mainly in Milan

Shortly after VE day in May 1945, I was ordered to Milan in the north of Italy. Milan was designated by the authorities as the main centre for the return of all the Middle East forces and it was decided that a chaplain was necessary, based on the English church of All Saints. So obeying orders I left 103 General Hospital and Muriel, knowing I would probably not see her again for perhaps another year.

Milan and its magnificent cathedral

The system of demobilisation from the Army after the war was 'first in first out'. In 1939, when war seemed almost inevitable, Muriel joined the Red Cross and trained as a nurse. Consequently she was called up immediately war was declared, and so now she returned to England to be demobbed soon after the war ended. She then had to wait in England for my return which was to be in the following March.

However, before she left Italy Muriel managed a week's leave from 103 General and hitchhiked up to Milan to see me, arriving at All Saints church in Milan just as I arrived to take the Sunday morning service. Her return to the hospital and to duty was not as smooth as we had arranged or anticipated. I had booked a passage on the Al Italia airline to take her back to Naples, but on arrival at the airport on the day of her departure we were told the flight was cancelled and that nothing was going to Naples that day. 'Absence without leave' is a serious offence, and Muriel was more than a little agitated. Just then a high-ranking staff officer came up and said, "Did I hear you wanted to go to Naples? There's a spare seat in my plane and you're welcome to it." So a miracle took place and Muriel was airlifted back to Naples and then taken in a staff car to the hospital at Nocera.

When I left 103 General Hospital to take up my job in Milan, I left with nothing but the happiest of memories and loved all my time there, as well, of course, as having the blessing of meeting my future wife. From the hospital at Nocera to Milan is a long journey, and I spent the first night in Rome and then a night in Florence and finally reached my destination and took up residence. How fortunate I had been in being able to visit so many different places, and all my travels were very enjoyable. On arrival in Milan I was told to book myself into the Hotel Tourismo, and found myself living permanently in a hotel for the first time in my life. I made my way to All Saints church and prepared for the next Sunday services. Milan is an industrial city rather like Manchester in England. Various representatives live there and the population includes many Italian wives or husbands who met their partners through their business associations. When Italy declared war, Anglo-Italians were liable to be interned and many fled to the mountains and stayed there until hostilities were over. On the first few Sundays at All Saints Church many fresh faces appeared and I got to know many Italians and their families. I've kept in touch with several of them and continue to do so right up until now.

From the church we organised a choir and I took the choir with me when I went to the radio station to broadcast a short service on Sunday evenings. This was called 'The Padre Looks In'. Lake Como is near Milan and I had many visits there to enjoy the spellbinding beauty of the lake and its environs. There is another English church on the lakeside at Cadenabia and I took services there as well as in Milan, and I also travelled to other military units in the area. Chaplains were called to a conference at Rapallo on the Italian Riviera on the shores of the Mediterranean. This is another beautiful area and for me yet another enjoyable experience. One of the

Cadenabia on Lake Como

members of the congregation at All Saints owned a flat on a farm at Gravedonna far up the lake near the Swiss border, and in later years we spent holidays in what was yet another scenic paradise.

On my first Remembrance Sunday in Milan, and the first after the end of the war, we organised a service in the largest cinema, and I prepared the details of the service and the lesson reader. On the Saturday evening I had a message from the General Officer Commanding informing me that he, the General, would be attending the service and he would read the lesson. I had already arranged and rehearsed someone to do the reading and said so.

Then came an order for me to report to the General at once, which I did, and was told by him that the tradition of the British Army was that the lesson is always read by the senior officer present, and he was going to be present so therefore he would read. I knew he had not intended coming to the service, but when he heard it was going to be broadcast had changed his mind and decided to attend. I told him I had already arranged everything for the service and prepared the lesson reader. All to no avail. He was coming and he would read! I was still in the Army, and just had to obey orders, albeit with a very bad grace. Next day the service was held and the cinema was packed with hundreds of men, many of whom had lost former comrades in action.

I had time to explore the city of Milan with its wonderful cathedral, the famous painting of the Last Supper and its fine and lovely shopping arcade. In the centre of the town was a Church Army canteen, which was extremely popular with the forces, and it was run by a Mrs Thomson, the former wife of the vicar of St Peter's, Eaton Square, in West London. In one of the many strange things which took place in the blitz, a bomb dropped on the vicarage and her husband was killed but she was unharmed. She then volunteered to work for the Church Army and did wonderful service working in canteens at various centres. In Milan, Mrs Thomson was very popular and did yeoman service. I visited the canteen regularly and took an epilogue there each Sunday evening. When I left to return to England I was presented with a triptych of the Cistine Madonna, and as I write I can see it opposite me on my bookcase. Alongside it there is a cross and candlesticks, which were bought for me when I first joined the Oxford and Bucks Light Infantry at Westwood Ho in 1940. I carried them with me all through the years of the war, and used them at every service whenever I set up shop, and wherever that happened to be.

During the time I served in Milan I was promoted to Senior Chaplain. It didn't really mean much, but you may know that an Army Chaplain has the rank of Captain and Senior Chaplains are promoted to Major. The insignia of the Army rank of Major is a crown worn on each shoulder. One of the officers sent me a card with the words of a hymn:

> *"Ye servants of the Lord.*
> *Each in his office wait.*
> *O happy servant he*
> *In such a posture found.*
> *He shall his Lord with rapture see,*
> *And be with honour crowned!"*

On discharge the gratuity awarded to service people is based on the person's rank, so what I received was a bonus which was rather more than I deserved but most useful when settling down in our new home after demob.

The time came for me to bid farewell to Milan and my life in the Army. I had much enjoyed caring for the church and the people, both military and civilian, in the city of Milan. According to the very good system of 'first in first out', I was due for demobilisation in March 1946 and I left by train for England on March 10th and travelled to Calais and from there to Dover. At the Army base at Aldershot many of us were being discharged and all of us reported to the quartermaster's stores to be kitted out with demobilisation everyday suitable clothes. Much scorn was poured on these garments, but I think it was rather unfair because clothing was rationed in England, and the citizens of our country had clothing coupons to cope with, as well as ration books for food, furniture, household goods and all utilities. Overseas personnel returned to our home country to find it badly scarred by bombsites and nearly financially bankrupt. Six years of war and much suffering had left its mark, and there were several more years of hardship still to come.

On being demobbed, all former Service people are given a travel pass to the destination of their choice. Muriel at that time was staying with her sister Marion in Purley, so she told me to get my pass for Purley Oaks. I duly got my pass for Purley Oaks, the station nearest to where Muriel's sister lived, and travelled up to London where Muriel met me at Waterloo Station. When she saw the pile of luggage I'd got with me, she said we would need a taxi and one cannot get a taxi from Purley Oaks, so we would have to go on one stop further to the main station at Purley. At Purley station we came to the barrier and the ticket collector looked at my pass, saw it was made out for Purley Oaks, and said, "Tuppence to pay." So after four years overseas, and going half way round the world, I duly paid the sum of tuppence in order to return home!

At some time during my service in the Army, I was 'Mentioned in Dispatches'. I have no recollection of what this was for, but it is awarded for distinguished service.

By the KING'S Order the name of
The Reverend H.G.Ockwell,
Royal Army Chaplains' Department,
was published in the London Gazette on
20 November, 1945,
as mentioned in a Despatch for distinguished service.
I am charged to record
His Majesty's high appreciation.

J.J. Lawson

Secretary of State for War

Muriel had been demobbed many months before me, and went back to her pre-war job at the Swiss Bank Corporation in the City. She also had quite a lot to do on our joint behalf because the Bishop of Southwark was aware of my intending return from Service and wished to appoint me Vicar of St Philip's Lambeth in Kennington Road, not far from Westminster Bridge and Lambeth Palace. When the date of my arrival from overseas was known, my institution as vicar was fixed for April 23rd 1946, six weeks after my return to England. Muriel was informed of the forthcoming arrangements at St Philip's and went to inspect the vicarage which was situated alongside the church. It had five floors: a basement and top floor not in use, the kitchen and dining room on the ground floor, a study and sitting room on the first floor, and three bedrooms and a bathroom on the second floor - a bit like living in a castle! Much needed to be done, such as measuring for curtains and getting necessary items before moving in.

Muriel did splendid work before I came home and our first task together was to try and obtain furniture. Of course we did not possess any, so we went to the Civil Service Stores in the Strand. We were able to buy almost everything we needed from their store of second hand goods, which were duly delivered and everything was made ready for our arrival in our first house. Before this happened, we had to make preparations for our wedding, which was fixed for April 2nd at St Matthew's, New Kent Road, the church I had served before I joined the Army. Invitations had to be sent out and all the necessary regulation things take place both for ourselves and for our new home, as well as arrangements for the reception after the service and for our honeymoon. Having been away for four years, and both of us not having any holiday for a long time, we felt justified in taking three weeks, so we fixed up to go to the Spread Eagle Hotel in Midhurst for the first week, to a hotel in Llandudno in North Wales for the second, and lastly to Blossoms Hotel in Chester for the final week.

Everything was prepared and the great day of the wedding arrived, and all went as planned, with our families and guests surrounding us. My ministry at St Matthew's, which began in 1936, officially came to an end with my marriage in 1946. I remember little about the actual wedding day and the joy of it, except the send-off after the reception and our journey to Midhurst. It was Springtime, and I loved the walks we had with the fresh green and spring flowers everywhere. We were recommended to go to the Spread Eagle Hotel because they said the food was good. This turned out to be untrue, but the next place in Wales made up for it. It was less than a year after the war ended and we needed to realise that excuses for many things had to be made because things were not yet anywhere near up to normal standards. We had a wonderful stay in Wales, climbing mountains and exploring the area. We'd been warned that Wales was often very wet, so we took wet weather precautions. In fact, we hung our up macs and things in the wardrobe when we arrived and there they stayed for the whole time of our holiday. The weather was perfect and very warm, and we shed warm clothing at every stage.

For the final week we took ourselves off to Chester. I'd wanted to return to Chester after staying at the teacher training college when I was first called up in 1940 and I loved the city and the cathedral. We stayed at the well-known Blossoms Hotel and joined in the services at the cathedral. In the hotel vestibule there was a notice board giving details of local amenities, cinema programmes and so on. At the weekend, just before we left, all the notices were changed for the coming week, but on the Tuesday, the day we left for London, the notice giving details for next Sunday's services still showed the times for the previous Sunday. I've never forgotten it and felt it gave the impression that the Church, as usual, instead of giving the lead was running along behind. Not altogether fair criticism but unfortunately only too true in many instances.

Lambeth Walk

Our honeymoon was over and back we went to London to take up residence in the vicarage of St Phillip's, Kennington Road. The house is in the main thoroughfare between Westminster Bridge and Kennington Oval, and buses and trams stopped right outside the front door. The trams in London were scrapped not long afterwards, but while we lived there they ran all night except between 2am and 4am. At this early morning hour the conduits in the middle of the tramlines, from which the power came to run the trams (there were no overhead lines), were cleaned out by a machine which flashed a strong light and made a horrible 'whoosh' as it went along. On the day we moved in, we were so tired we slept through the noise and never really noticed it. From then on, whenever we had visitors we would ask them in the morning if they'd slept well and received a very old fashioned look, because they had been woken by this noise and light outside!

Hopping on a bus or a tram to go into town was a regular happening, and I used to go to the Strand to get my hair cut which at that time cost me 1/6d (7 ½ new pence). Fancy that in the heart of the West End! Things have changed a great deal since then – my income at that time was £8 a week. Two days after taking up residence at the vicarage and starting our new life together I was instituted by the Bishop of Southwark as vicar of the Parish of St Philip with the accompanying job as Chaplain of Lambeth Hospital. Like other parts of London, the parish had been bombed quite badly and the church and the parish hall needed much rebuilding and redecoration, so the task was one of rebuilding the church and renewing the congregation. All the usual fundraising activities took place and gradually things began to improve. The stonemasons got to work, and soon we were able to hold a thanksgiving service for the restoration of the building.

Lambeth hospital is situated less than ½ a mile away from St Philip's church. I'd been a patient there after being bombed in September 1940 and now I found myself their chaplain. The buildings had been built as a Victorian Workhouse and consisted of several large blocks spread over a wide area in concrete yards, and there was also a small Chapel. Every Sunday morning I held a communion service at 6.30am for members of the staff, and then took sick communions round the wards for people who had asked for it when I visited the day before. This meant running up and down flights of stairs and arriving by the bedside of patients trying to look as if I had all the time in the world. After this I went back for the 8 o'clock service at St Phillip's, and had to put my feet up in the vestry to recover my strength before taking it. I was aged 34 and now I wonder how I managed to do what I did.

During our stay at Lambeth, Andrew and Timothy were born at Lambeth Hospital. The matron of the hospital became a great friend, as did the medical superintendent, and I received much help with my ministry from them. One day I came face to face with the Archbishop of Canterbury, geoffrey Fisher, as he came out from one of the wards. When I asked the ward sister if she had seen her very important visitor she was completely unaware of his presence. His chauffeur was an inpatient after an operation for appendicitis, and the archbishop had come to visit him as one might expect, but with no pomposity of any kind. On subsequent occasions when I met him he was always friendly, and with no side, and so also was his wife, Rosamund. I invited Mrs Fisher to come and present the prizes at our church school and afterwards she came into the vicarage and had tea with us. She enquired from Muriel where she took the children when she went for a walk with them, and Muriel told her she walked over Lambeth Bridge and went to St James Park. "You don't want to do that," said Mrs Fisher. "You don't need to walk that far. I'll arrange for you to use the gate of the Palace Gardens and you can come and go as you please." This she did, and thereafter Muriel had a very much shorter journey.

One or two things stand out at during our stay at St Phillips. At the time, Danny Kaye was all the rage, especially with young people. He was appearing at the London Palladium and since the young people of the parish were all talking about him, we thought we ought to go and see him ourselves, but everyone said, "You'll never get a ticket – they were all sold out long ago." I reported this to my curate, Mark Shirley, whom it so happened was an enthusiastic playgoer and wrote reviews for new shows for the parish magazine. I told him I wanted to go and see Danny Kaye but couldn't get tickets. He said, "Go to the Army and Navy Stores in Victoria Street." I did so and asked for two tickets for the Palladium. "Yes sir, what seats would you like?" said the shop assistant. It appears that places such as the Army and Navy Stores block-book tickets for shows and their clients benefit from this arrangement, so I was able to get the tickets and see the show.

It is also the case that unsold tickets at theatres are offered to nearby hospitals a day or two before the performance, and sometimes the Matron of Lambeth Hospital would ring us up and offer them to us if we were free and able to use them. Accordingly we went to many shows which we would never have seen in normal circumstances. One in particular stands out in my mind, and that was 'Ann Frank'. In all my life, before or since, I have never been to a performance where at the end, instead of applause, there was absolute silence. It was most moving and unforgettable.

About 18 months after I became Vicar I began to feel very unwell and for a few days did no visiting. When I began to feel better I decided to make my normal visit to the church school, but next day I was even worse in health and seemed to have pain all over my body. The doctor came and I was admitted to Lambeth Hospital. The cause was mumps! I had not suffered this usually childhood complaint, and now it affected just about all of me and I was extremely unwell. Everyone asking after my health thought it was quite amusing that the Vicar had mumps - for me it was anything but funny.

One day, one of the magazine distributors came back from his round and informed me that Mrs Coombs did not want the magazine any more, so I asked him to call again next month and find out the reason why. He did so, and came and told me she'd said she had been in hospital and the vicar had never come to see her. It turned out that I was in hospital with mumps at the same time that she was there. No more copies of the magazine for Mrs Coombs! It's an extraordinary thing that when the doctor is needed he's sent for, but the vicar or rector is expected to have second sight and find out for himself. Time and again, when people have complained about not having a visit, I have said I did not know they were in need, only for them to say, "I thought you were sure to know."

While visiting in my parish I came across a very poor

but attractive family living in deplorable conditions, and this worried me a great deal. I felt we had rooms in the vicarage which we did not use, and after discussing it with Muriel we decided to offer accommodation to Mr and Mrs Almeida and their two children. They could have the spacious basement as their living quarters and use the top floor for bedrooms. There would be no charge, as Mrs Almeida would help Muriel with cleaning etc. The arrangement was agreed and the family moved in and they stayed with us for the rest of the time I was Vicar.

In our first days of marriage Muriel was somewhat taken aback by my absence in the evenings. She expected what is, or was, the normal domestic pattern of the husband being at work all day and back home in the evening, but the life of a parish priest does not work out that way. Youth groups, wedding preparations, parish events, confirmation classes and all kinds of things take place in the evenings. However, I was home in the morning and for lunch, so really and truly it was like turning the day upside down. I was home each day and out each evening.

The matron of Lambeth Hospital (where Andrew and Timothy were born) became a friend of the family and made much of Andrew in his early years. She had a flat in the hospital, and Andrew went and stayed with her on several occasions. She spoilt him in a big way, and one day he returned home and said, "I wish I lived with Mamie" (as he called her) "and only came and stayed with you!" He was very bad at eating his dinner and was told one day to stay at the table until he had finished. In a short while he appeared in the kitchen with a clean plate and was commended for being a good boy. The same thing happened the next day. Then came the time for the fireplace to be cleaned and behind an electric stove were the remains of the dinners he had supposedly eaten.

People of a different colour were at that time very rare in England. I had invited an African preacher one Sunday, and as is the usual custom he stayed behind afterwards for lunch. Just before the start of the meal Muriel scolded Andrew for not washing his hands. He looked across the table at our guest and exclaimed, "Well he hasn't washed his!" On another occasion we were invited out to tea and the hostess had prepared a very good spread. Andrew took a sandwich and a bite from it and exclaimed, "This bread is stale." "Shhh," "Well I don't like stale bread." "Sshhh" "Well it is stale." "Ssshhh". Imagine our embarrassment also when we went to a 'do' and a splendid array of good things had been prepared. Andrew looked at it all and said, "There is nothing here I like." From this you may realise that vicarage children are exactly the same as any other children, and we had plenty of experiences of a similar kind in the future. Very amusing in retrospect, but not at the time.

Part of a parish priest's ministry is to take holy communion to the sick and house-bound, and I went regularly to see a lovely old lady who was just on 89 years of age, a Mrs Evans, who lived in a miserable bedsit. The view from her window was of the grey slates on the roof of the house next door. Looking back I can't think why we didn't do more to improve her lot. Just before her 90th birthday she fell out of bed and fractured her femur and landed up in Lambeth Hospital. I went to see her and she said, "I think my time has come, vicar." I said it was quite possible this was true, but she had nothing to worry about, and I said the 23rd Psalm and the Lord's Prayer with her, and left her quietly composed and happy, and I then moved to talk to the woman in the next bed.

At that moment Mrs Evans' daughter arrived and her mother said to her just what she had said to me. The daughter exclaimed, "Nonsense mother, you'll be better tomorrow!" Why, I wonder, do we try and pretend that death will not happen rather than try and help old people to die with dignity? Mrs Evans did die, and we mourned her loss and thanked God for her at the funeral service at St Phillip's.

All clergy get many callers asking for money, food or some other form of help, and hard-luck stories abound. I made it a rule never to give money, but always offer food and drink. I could fill a book with the tales we were told, and I began to ask where people lived. I got the same address, that of a bombed site, over and over again. I knew the address well, and said, "I am going that way later on and will call in and see you." This was met with, "Please do not trouble yourself", and I would reply that it was no trouble at all!

Clergy also get very many letters asking for help from numerous charities – two or even three or four arrive by post almost every day. People must think clergy are a soft touch! I decided it was best not to give a small amount to a large number of charities, but give as much as possible to three or four. So for many years I have supported the Children's Society, Christian Aid, Water Aid and a child in Egypt, as well as contributing to my parish church.

St Philip's parish hall was equipped with a stage and a set of footlights which were raised above the level at the front, and one day I jumped over the lights, a thing I had done many times before, landed awkwardly, and managed to damage my ankle quite badly. No more tennis or strenuous activities for a long period, and I learned always to put my left foot forward when climbing a stile or anything similar. Laid up for some while, I wondered how to use my time and not get too bored with the forced inactivity. I remembered that one of the parishioners was employed at Buckingham Palace as an upholsterer. Apparently his job was to see that all chairs and other items of furniture were 100% immaculate, and before a State occasion he went round and made certain all was well. I rang him up and asked him to call round, and when he came I said, "I can use my hands if not my legs", so would he show me how to reupholster our dining room chairs which badly needed it. He did so and showed me the tricks of the trade. I still use my knowledge of this craft and have found it very useful over and over again.

The Bishop of Southwark had his office just up the road from the vicarage, because in 1940 the Army had requisitioned Bishop's House and they still hung on to it, so he had to find alternative accommodation. This meant he often 'popped in' to ask Muriel if she would provide a few cakes or biscuits for a meeting he had arranged in his office. Bertram Simpson was a much beloved Bishop and he baptised all four of our children, Andrew, Timothy, Rachel and James. He was a great preacher and I still remember one of his sermons on "Are you a pilgrim or a tramp?" It was said he was the late Queen Mary's favourite preacher and I can well believe it.

One of the tasks of being a vicar in the Deanery of Lambeth was the necessity of taking part in a rota system for burials at Lambeth Cemetery. This was because all the churchyards of inner London had long since been filled and London boroughs had to find land for cemeteries on the outskirts of the city. As one travels to London by train, these vast cemeteries can be seen as one approaches the main line stations. Lambeth Cemetery is actually at Tooting. In parishes containing many thousands of people funerals are not uncommon, and if every parish priest travelled to the cemetery for each burial from his parish it would mean all their time would be taken up 'toing and froing'. So the plan was for the burial service to take place in the parish church, and then at the cemetery the duty chaplain would take the internment. Not an ideal arrangement, but the only thing possible in the circumstances.

When my turn came, each morning for one week I went by tram to Tooting and walked the half-mile to the cemetery bringing sandwiches and coffee with me to sustain me through the day. None of us clergy like taking services for people we do not know, but it has to be done. One day, at the time of an epidemic, I took 13, and altogether 58 services by the end of the week. It is hard to be 'fresh' repeating the same words over and over again, but I have tried to behave at each funeral (or wedding) by reminding myself that for this family there is only one funeral or wedding and this is it, and I have sought to impress this on every curate who has assisted me in parish work.

I used to get quite 'worked up about funerals because there were 1st, 2nd, 3rd and 'Common Grave' arrangements. The poorer you were the meaner the arrangements. Common graves were often about a mile from the main gate and I have seen more than 20 small memorial stones on one plot. Fortunately all that is now history, as cremation has become almost the norm. What would have happened if it were not so, I don't know. Lambeth Cemetery was almost full 50 years ago, and that

London Borough and others would have had to reach out for more land 20 miles or so from the centre of London. We were not exactly well off during our stay at St Philips. My stipend was £400 a year, which meant the necessity for economy in everyday living. For instance we had coffee once a week and tea on other days because coffee was too expensive for us to have it daily. Muriel used to take items of used clothing to a second-hand clothes shop along the road and sell things to raise funds. Charity shops did not exist then and today's abundance of cheap and good ready-made clothing was a dream for the future. We were quite severely rationed for several years after the war and for some things it was worse than in wartime. Our meat ration for the week was ten pennyworth, just about enough for one small meal. One day I tried to carve our weekly joint and found it nothing but fat and gristle. I picked up the dish and carried it down the road to the butcher's shop, showed it to him and asked how we were supposed to exist for a week on that. He said nothing but took the dish from me, tipped the lot in a bucket, and gave me the best piece of steak we had had for a very long time.

For our summer holidays we undertook a 'locum tenens', which means that the local incumbent goes away on holiday leaving his home and his duties to another priest who comes and spends his holiday there. We had many happy days at places we could not otherwise have afforded to visit and in various parts of the country - Devon, Shropshire, Essex, Lincolnshire, Norfolk, Kent and so on. Later, when I had no assistant curate myself, we advertised for a locum to come and take over in our parish. The system works very well.

Surbiton Special

Six years in Lambeth went swiftly by, and by this time the church was fully restored and the congregation expanding. Then the Bishop asked me to become vicar of St Andrew's Surbiton, a very different type of parish from Lambeth. My assistant curate took my Sunday morning services for me at St Philip's while I went to spy out the land at St Andrew's in order to help me make up my mind whether to become the vicar there or not. In spite of the terrible weather that day, the congregation was good and the interior of the church very impressive. So after some days of thought and prayer I agreed to move and plans were made to bring this about.

The outgoing vicar was Dick Cartwright who was leaving to become vicar of St Mary Redcliffe, Bristol. Afterwards he became bishop of Plymouth. At my ordination service way back in 1936, Dick and I walked side by side and we have kept in touch with each other ever since. He told me St Andrew's was a very good living as the stipend was £600 a year! A few years later Mervyn Stockwood, who had become Bishop of Southwark, held a synod in the cathedral and informed us that one of his ambitions was to raise the stipend of incumbents to £1000 a year. It seemed then like untold riches.

Leaving St Philip's parish meant leaving the vicarage which was also the home of the Almeida family. What could be done about them? I got in touch with various estate agents and obtained a very pleasant flat near the Elephant and Castle, certainly better than anything the Almeidas had ever had before. When I told Mrs Almeida we were leaving and they also had to move but that I had obtained a flat for them, she asked where the flat was. When I told her she exclaimed in a shocked voice, "The Elephant and Castle!" It was an amazing fact that strong social distinctions existed between different areas of London. This flat was only about a mile away from St Philip's vicarage. Anyway, they had to go when we did and later on I visited them in their new home to find that they had settled in happily and all manner of things were well.

So we were off to Surbiton with our two small boys, Andrew aged five and Timothy, two (Rachel was born in 1953 in Surbiton Hospital, and James in Kingston Hospital in 1959). The induction at St Andrew's took place in January 1962 and we began a very happy ten years.

Surbiton is mostly a Victorian suburb and I believe owes its growth to the coming of the railway. The main line to and from Waterloo and Portsmouth would have been laid through Kingston-on-Thames – an ancient town with a market place and many historical connections, but the people there at the time would not have anything to do with 'this new fangled invention' so the line was pushed away and a station built at Surbiton. There is

St Andrew's, Surbiton

now a wonderful train service to London, the journey taking only 12 minutes, and because of it, Surbiton has grown to its present size.

No doubt the residents of Kingston-on-Thames wish their forebears had been rather more agreeable to the coming of the railway. Nowadays we have much trouble when new major roads and bypasses are suggested, but when the multitude of train lines were laid in the 19th century they cut across farms and just about everything. My uncle's farm had the Great Western Railway cutting across it, but all that happened was the building of a tunnel under the railway line and the cattle wandered from one field to the other. Stations, bridges, tunnels everywhere, and today we take them all for granted as if they had always been there.

Later on, when I became rector of Blendworth, Chalton and Idsworth, I discovered that the owners of Idsworth House refused to have the railway line crossing the drive leading to their house, and so the home was moved to its present site! The line of trees leading up the hill to where the old house was situated can still be seen to this day.

The expanding population of Surbiton gave rise to the building of four new churches - St Mark's, with a daughter church of St Andrew, Christ Church and St Matthew's. At some point St Andrew's became a separate parish, but it is now once again grouped with St Mark's. The church building is a large red brick edifice with a rather strange shaped tower. The exterior is not particularly pleasing to the eye but the interior is spacious and during the incumbency of Dick Cartwright alterations were made which gave it a splendid kind of beauty, and it lent itself to a high standard of worship which was its hallmark.

When we arrived there was a Sung Eucharist on Sundays at 11.15 and an outstanding choir of men and boys singing a different setting of the music for the service every Sunday. Alongside this service a new order had just come into being, a Parish Communion service at 9 a.m., which was less formal but part of a growing movement in which the Holy Communion service is the centre of worship. 9 a.m. seems early on a Sunday morning, but social habits were changing, mostly because of the arrival of the motorcar. People could now journey out and engage in all kinds of pastimes, having already attended a service at an hour that did not take up the whole morning. Within our few years at Surbiton, the 9 a.m. service would become full to overflowing, while the 11.15 continued but did not attract newcomers.

In Lambeth I had the help of a curate and a woman worker, and now at Surbiton I had two curates plus a new deacon. This meant we were able to do quite a lot together as a team, and I benefited from their assistance. We tried to visit everyone in the parish and delivered leaflets a week beforehand saying one of the clergy would be visiting at such-and-such a time on such-and-such a day and if they did not wish for a visit, or if another time would be more suitable, please to let us know. By this means we covered a lot of ground, and no-one was able to say, "I've lived here for many years and nobody from the church has ever been to see me".

The parish hall had been destroyed during the war and so we did everything possible to get it rebuilt. At that time a licence was necessary before any building work could take place but after many months of pressure on various government and council departments we got approval for our plans and work began on a new parish hall. At the time I asked the architect to design the stage along the lines of a West End of London theatre with all its fittings. In later years I came to the conclusion this was a mistake. In fact the stage was rarely used and the space could have been better utilised for various parish activities. One thing we did was to incorporate a flat above the stage area for a hall caretaker, and this proved a great blessing. Still more building work was undertaken at this time because there was great need for a new choir vestry and toilet facilities, and eventually these were built alongside the parish church.

Two years after our arrival the coronation of Queen Elizabeth 2nd took place and the service was televised for the first time in history. Then, not many had television sets, and those who did organised parties so that as many as possible could see this wonderful occasion. Almost everyone managed to watch it, but none of us from the vicarage. Afterwards everyone was talking about it and we had to say we had not seen it. Again and again people said, "If only we had known you could have come to us, but we were sure you would have been invited somewhere." Later on we did see the service on the big screen at the cinema.

The choir at St Andrew's, under the direction of 'Polly' Perkins, was splendid and the general standard of music very high, but the organ left much to be desired. We heard that a very good instrument was 'going begging' at a bombed church at Stroud Green in north London and could be had for free if we paid for its removal, the carriage and its rebuilding at St Andrew's. Off we went to see it, and Mr Perkins was able to creep into the bombed church and play the organ - softly, softly, because we were told that the roof might collapse if loud music caused vibration. Back we went to Surbiton, quite sure the instrument would be a great asset to the worship and musical tradition of St Andrew's, and arrangements were made to dispose of our old organ. The various parts of the organ from Stroud Green were carted across London and set up in our parish church, and there it still is, and still gives pleasure to many people. During the time of the removal of the old and installation of the new organ, all services were accompanied on a grand piano.

Congregations were always extremely good and on occasions such as the Three Hour service on Good Friday it was remarkable in total number. A priest I knew well, called McGreggor Lewis, had been one of the lecturers along with me at Southwark Diocesan Summer School. He was wonderful with young people and as we say, 'they would eat out of his hand'. He was extremely well thought of, and I invited him to come and take the Three Hours one Good Friday at St Andrew's. He agreed to come if I would swap with him and take his service at St James, Camberwell, where he was vicar. We agreed on this arrangement and because of his reputation I expected a flourishing Good Friday congregation when I went, but in this vast Victorian building we had five people for the first hour, three for the second and got up to nine for the third hour. I kept reminding those present of all the hundreds of people who were joining with us all over the country and in many parts of the world.

The fact was McGreggor Lewis should never have been a parish priest. He was a marvellous lecturer and teacher and his excellent gifts should have been used in some other way. After a Three Hours service it is the custom for the visiting conductor to be offered refreshments, and on this occasion I went to the vicarage and was given a dreadful fish pie and then asked if I would like a cup of tea. I said, "Please, but no sugar," whereupon the vicar's wife poured one out, put sugar in it and drank it herself! They were a wonderful pair but square pegs in round holes.

In the congregation we had an old lady called Mrs Broom. She was always dressed in black and was therefore known as Black Broom. She came regularly to Evensong each day, always arrived late, and usually managed to knock something over. One day at Evensong a series of incidents took place which caused Gavin Cooper, one of the curates, to stop what he was saying, and all of us could hardly contain ourselves for laughing. I told our children we must be kind to Black Broom because she could not help her oddities and was not quite right in the head. My intention was to be kind, but next day we met her in the road and Andrew exclaimed, "Is that the old lady who Dad said is not quite right in the head?" Fortunately, I don't think she heard! When she died she left me all her money and possessions. The money totalled about £100, and after all the expenses were paid I received just a few shillings, but she meant well and it was very heart warming.

One of the curates, Martin Brown, with his wife Shelagh, had two small girls, and one afternoon there was a 'do' in the vicarage garden. The lawn had a raised edge and the children were jumping on it in places and breaking it down. If you have ever had a similar lawn you will know how difficult it is to carry out repairs, so I asked the children to stop the game they were playing because of the damage. A week later one of the children said to her mother, "The vicar told us to keep away from the edges". "Oh," said Shelagh. "And did you?" "No," said the small girl, "but we kept away from the vicar!" A similar event happened a few years later. James was riding round the garden on a small tricycle and at the time we had some friends staying with us with their small son Andrew. Muriel went up to James and told him to let Andrew have a turn on the tricycle. Very reluctantly James got off, let Andrew go once round the garden, then went up to him and said, "Tea's ready."

The chaplaincy of Tolworth Hospital went with the job of vicar of St Andrew's. Tolworth is on the other side of Surbiton, and I do not know how this arrangement came to be. The hospital was for TB patients and this meant they were all 'long stay', and I was able to build real relationships with them. Every Sunday evening I arranged for the Youth Fellowship to come with me and we held a service in the wards. The young people took part in the prayers, and after the service would go round and talk to the patients. One of them was the sister of Petula Clark, a very well known popular singer all those years ago. The matron of the hospital was known to me because Briony Moffett had been a sister at 103 General Hospital where I served as chaplain during the war, so we had much in common. When I arrived in Surbiton, Tolworth Hospital was full of patients with TB, but by the time I left, ten years later, only two inmates had TB and the rest were geriatric cases. TB was almost wiped out through the advent of new drugs, and because of these and other advances in medicine, more and more people are living to a great age, needing more and more care and attention and filling many beds in our hospitals and care homes.

One of the members of the PCC at St Andrew's was a barrister and seemed always to treat other people as if they were 'in the dock'. I found it very trying and things rather came to a head as we approached out AGM. Someone quietly told me that Mr H was going to challenge me on some point of legal order. I carefully looked up all the relevant details so as to be ready if it should happen. Sure enough it did, and he rose to say that what I was proposing was illegal. I replied, saying, "It is not illegal Mr H, and I sometimes wonder what you would feel like if I kept telling you how to do your job in the same way that you seem to think you can tell me how to do mine." There was an awful silence before we continued.

Next morning a letter was put through the vicarage door saying he was resigning from the PCC, and informing me that I had achieved what seemed to be the object of all the clergy, and that was the silence of the laity. The family - mother, father and their daughters - left St Andrew's and went to a neighbouring parish church each Sunday, but after a year or so, quietly returned and there was no more trouble. Human beings, which of course includes me, are a funny lot! One regular member of the congregation did not appear for two or three weeks so I called to see if she was unwell. I was greeted very frostily on the doorstep with, "I go to a church where I can sit where I like". What had happened was that at a weekday service I had asked everyone to sit together in the front half of the church. She sat, as she always did, right at the back, so I had gone to her and said, "Won't you come and join us further forward?" Ah well!

Life at St Andrew's was never dull, and as well as the visiting at Tolworth Hospital I was asked by the Bishop of Southwark to represent the diocese on the Metropolitan Regional Hospital Board. He said the Bishop of Kingston had been doing this task but wished to retire, and because of my experience as hospital chaplain in the war, then at

Lambeth and now at Tolworth, he wanted me to undertake it. The Hospital Board consisted of representatives from the dioceses of Canterbury, Guildford, Portsmouth, Chichester, Southwark, Winchester and Salisbury. We met at the London headquarters of the Metropolitan Board in Paddington several times a year. The real responsibility was to visit hospitals in each area and meet the chaplain and the matron, inspect the chapel and the mortuary and generally try and make sure the spiritual care of patients was properly attended to as part of the healing ministry of the hospital. The secretary of the Regional Hospital Board made all the arrangements for the day and time of visits.

This work proved very interesting, and led to an event which stands out in my memory. At one particular hospital, the chaplain greeted me by saying, "Do you know anyone who would like to do this job?" He was obviously a misfit there, but the same man would later become famous as the founder of the important national organisation called The Samaritans.

One day, I was on my way to visit Richmond Hospital and stopped my car at the top of Richmond Hill in order to look at the very lovely view. As I got out of the car, I came face to face with a man who exclaimed, "Hello, Sir! I haven't seen you since we were in the desert in North Africa 20 years ago." I asked him if he lived in Richmond, and he said, "No, I live in Newcastle." I asked how he came to be in Richmond, and he told me he had come to London on holiday and at Westminster Bridge had seen a notice advertising a boat trip on the Thames to Richmond. He decided to take the trip, and this was how we had met up with each other again after all those years – an astounding coincidence.

During my time at Surbiton I did two spells as mayor's chaplain. As is the case in the House of Commons, each session starts with a prayer by the chaplain, and each session of the Borough Council in Surbiton began with a prayer by the mayor's chaplain. This duty, among others, taught me quite a lot about the workings of local government. I remember, for example, becoming aware of the fact that a plan to build more homes meant enlarging the sewage works. Most of us are probably like me and do not even think about what happens to our waste products. In this particular case, more homes meant more sewage than the existing works could cope with. Another side of the office of chaplain made me more and more convinced of the folly of bringing local government into the political arena. To vote on local problems according to which party one supports seemed to me then, and still does, absurd.

The clergy of the Diocese of Southwark elected me to serve as a member of the Canterbury Convocation and the Church Assembly (now the General Synod), so off I went to Westminster for the opening session. It was quite something to be 'walking the corridors of power', but after a year or so I knew I was in the wrong place. There in Westminster were all the Bishops, Archdeacons, Deans and representatives from all over the country, but the business being conducted did not really excite me. I am an ordinary parish priest and felt I ought to be in the parish and not at Church House. So I served just one session of four or five years, and when I said I would not be standing for re-election some members said, "You will miss it, and you'll be standing again at the next by-election." I never did miss it, and was not tempted to return.

We went on holiday to do a 'locum' at Spilsby in

Lincolnshire, and chose this particular location because it was a completely new area to us. We were surprised at the flatness of the countryside and the fact that much of the coastal area is behind a sea wall. We knew all about the conditions of much of Holland, but did not realise how much of eastern England is similar to that country. Later on, as a result of this locum, I was asked to take a mission week at Alford and another one at Sleaford, both in Linclolnshire. Subsequently, I took missions at Emsworth in Hampshire and at Byfleet in Surrey. Looking back, I wonder how I had the nerve to accept the invitations, and hope my advent was not too much of a disappointment for the good folk in the parishes. The one at Emsworth took place when Muriel was nearing full term expecting our youngest child, James. I had no idea at the time that one day I would come to live in the district of Emsworth.

After the mission at Emsworth, and when I had returned to Surbiton, I became very unwell. Muriel went into Kingston Hospital to have the baby and James was born on November 10th 1959, but soon after I was too unwell to go and visit her. At the time we had Judith, aged 18, staying with us. She lived in Axminster in Devon, and her parents had asked Muriel's sister, Beryl, who was married to a priest and lived in that part of the world, if she thought we would look after Judith while she studied at the Royal College of Music in London.

While I was ill in bed Judith did her best to care for me, but soon decided to call the doctor. She came into the bedroom and said, "The doctor wants to know if you want to see him?" I shook my head; because at the time I did not want to see anybody. Muriel was due home with the new baby and she was told she could only come home on condition she did not come into the bedroom or anywhere near me. She duly arrived home with James, and spoke to me on the other side of the bedroom door. She at once realised that all was not well and rang the doctor, who when he came told Judith off for not getting him to come sooner. She stood up to him, and said, "You're the doctor, and you should know the vicar would not be in bed unless there was something really wrong with him." Within a short while an ambulance was at the door and I was off to Surbiton Hospital with double pneumonia. So James, the new baby, and Muriel came home from hospital and I departed to hospital on the same day.

Later on, when I had recovered, the good parishioners of St Andrew's decided I needed a period of convalescence, and without my knowledge fixed up for Muriel, the baby and me to stay for two weeks at a lovely hotel in Eastbourne. Absolutely everything was taken care of – travel to and fro and all expenses paid. Andrew, Tim and Rachel were fixed up to stay with different parishioners for as long as necessary.

St Andrew's people were a wonderful lot, and we were always well cared for and spent many happy years there. During our stay we organised a parish holiday to the Passion Play in Oberammergau which proved a great success in every way. The Oberammergau passion play takes place every ten years and the play is outstandingly moving and never to be forgotten. We went again ten years later and liked it even more. The scenery in that part of the world is most beautiful, and after the play we stayed on in Austria. The courier of our coach party asked me if he should arrange for the use of the Lutheran chapel for our Sunday services. I said, "Please do". He returned later and said he had been unable to contact anyone, and asked me if he should go and see about the possibility of using the

Roman Catholic church. I said he could try but I doubted if he would get much luck in that direction. Experience in England made this a natural response, but I could not have been more wrong. He returned and said the parish priest was most helpful and they would be delighted to welcome us. On the Sunday morning we arrived and I used their communion vessels, and before the service a nun helped me to vest. At that time their hospitality was more than a little unusual and was a wonderful exhibition of Christian charity.

The years in Surbiton went swiftly by, but not before a rather frightening episode in the vicarage. One morning, just before it was time to get up, we had quite a severe thunderstorm and several claps of thunder shook the house. We got up, and Muriel went into the children's bedroom next door. At that moment there was a roar, and the ceiling of our bedroom came down amidst clouds of dust and large portions of plaster fell all over everything. On the pillow, where Muriel's head had been just a few moments before, was a large heavy piece of the ceiling. Later, it was thought the ceiling had probably been loosened during the air raids of 39-45 and the vibration of the thunder had finally brought it down. Whatever the cause, it was a miracle that Muriel was unharmed, and for some time after we had to sleep in another room until a new ceiling was installed and the other ceilings tested.

We had wonderfully happy years in Surbiton, made many friends and received much kindness both for ourselves and our children (two when we arrived and now four). After ten years the bishop sent for me and said, "You will probably never speak to me again when you know what I want you to do." There had been many months of a public scandal that had ended with a parish priest being unfrocked, and the parish was badly in need of help and guidance. Several folk had been much hurt, and many had their faith undermined. "So," said the bishop, "I want you to go to the Ascension, Balham." I asked for a period so that I could think and pray about it, and went home to tell Muriel. She was hoping I was about to be offered some lovely parish in the country environs of the diocese, and could hardly refrain from tears when I told her what I had been asked to do –leave the happy and flourishing parish of St Andrew's and move back to inner London and take on this difficult job.

I went to see the church and parish, and remember standing in this large Victorian building and found myself saying out loud, "God help me." It was cold, dirty and generally depressing and had the feeling of being unloved, with an atmosphere somehow of a 'hangover' from all the unhappy doings of the previous 12 months. Leaving St Andrew's would be a big wrench, but of course I said 'yes' to the bishop, and the wheels were put in motion for our move to the Church of the Ascension, Balham Hill.

Hilltop

The vicarage was surprisingly attractive, with lofty rooms and a fair sized garden at the back. Over the garden wall were the playing fields of a school alongside Clapham Common. The Common has many large houses situated alongside its boundaries and these date back to the days of horse-drawn carriages. Before the advent of the motorcar, City merchants lived in properties that were within carriage distance of the City, and drove out over London Bridge as far as places like Clapham and Brixton. The headquarters of Surrey Cricket Club are at the Oval, which may well come as a surprise, but at the time the club was formed it would have been surrounded by green fields. The large houses surrounding Clapham Common have long since been converted into flats or service centres of one sort or another.

The bedrooms at the back of the vicarage look out over the school playing fields and the front of the house is directly opposite the church. A great deal of redecoration in the house was needed before we moved in and there was a need for a new heating system. Work was put in hand and I drove up to Balham to see how work was progressing. The workmen were very friendly and helpful, but warned me that the next-door neighbour was 'a right lot'. So it proved to be. Apparently he came round and complained to the workmen about everything he could think of. I decided that if he came to see me I would take the wind out of his sails and be ultra friendly and invite him in. Soon after we moved in, the bell rang and sure enough there he was. Before he could speak, I asked him in. What he came for I cannot remember, but my welcome made no difference and throughout our stay he was always complaining.

Later on, as part of a fund raising effort, we had a brick sale across the road and during it a policeman came to the door and said the next-door neighbour had complained we were obstructing the footpath. Since the said footpath was across the road in front of the church, it was a ridiculous complaint, and the policeman agreed with me. Similarly John Willard, our assistant curate, collected pieces of wood for a Guy Fawkes Day bonfire, which he was organising for the Youth Club, and he deposited some pieces of wood against the brick wall of the house next door. Not for long! Round came the neighbour to complain it would make his house damp. So it went on, and I found myself wondering if he spent all his time spying on us in order to find a reason to complain. What he got out of life I cannot imagine.

100 yards away from the vicarage, at the end of the road, was the Odeon Cinema, and because I wanted a sign fixed to the side wall of it directing people to the parish church, I made it my business to call on the manager. He was delighted to help and said if we ever wanted to see a film, tickets for us were always available – a privilege we used from time to time. The drawback with having the cinema, and also Clapham South Underground station nearby, was that people used the road where the vicarage and church were situated as a convenient place for car parking, and it was always full of cars, often blocking our garage entrance. On one occasion I needed to get the car out to drive to a funeral, and because it was blocked in had to get some strong men to manhandle my car out of the garage and into the road so that I could proceed. After many such difficulties, I took the law into my own hands

and painted white lines on the road outside, fully expecting to get into trouble for doing so, but nothing ever happened and thereafter I was able to get in and out of the garage without difficulty.

When the date was fixed for my institution as vicar of the Ascension, Balham Hill, we very sadly took our farewell of the beloved congregation and church of St Andrew's Surbiton and with a heavy heart moved back to inner London to a new life in this problem parish.

The Ascension, Balham

The induction service took place with a huge congregation present, because many came from Surbiton and people from surrounding parishes supported us. On our first Sunday morning, however, the total number present was just 33, which included five members of our own family. At St Andrew's we had a splendid choir of men and boys and averaged 400 communicants every week, so imagine the contrast. The Ascension Church held about 650, and our total of 33 was scattered about in dim religious light. At Evensong I said it was like taking a service on Clapham Junction Station on a foggy night, because the faithful were almost invisible at the back of the church.

So how to tackle the future? There were two things that needed attention – 1). Improve the general state of the church building, and 2). Build up the congregation. The latter occupied my thoughts at the beginning, and I decided on a three-year plan. In the first year there would be a School of Prayer, in the second year we would concentrate on learning more about our faith so as to give a reason for our membership, and we would prepare for and hold a Teaching Week. In the third year we would be concerned with a Parish Mission, going out to all the people of the parish. Plans were made for the total redecoration and re-ordering of the interior of the church building, and some pews were removed and various alterations were made. The lighting was improved, and in general the interior was transformed to the extent that a funeral director coming in for a funeral said he thought he had come to the wrong church!

One of the benefits of taking on the job at Balham was that I could do no wrong, and I did a great deal in a short time which in normal circumstances would probably have taken many years, or might never have been done at all. Along the roadside of the church was a hedge, and the local population found it just the place where rubbish could be thrown over and be unseen. So down came the hedge, and open iron railings were fitted. Thereafter there was no problem with unwanted junk. The garden was turned into a rose garden with roses planted in memory of departed loved ones, and later on part of it was dedicated by the Bishop of Kingston as a place for the burial of ashes after cremation.

I was fortunate in that I had tremendous help given

by Muriel who was a first class companion in every way and particularly in the circumstances at this time, and we also had three children who were at an age when they could make various contributions. Andrew and Timothy were immediately trained as servers, and soon others joined them. Rachel joined the choir, and choirboys and girls were recruited with the help of the headmaster of the local school. After the 9.15am sung Eucharist everyone was invited to come to the vicarage for parish breakfast in the dining room. Eventually we had to transfer to the parish hall and set up on Saturday evening for 60+ people. Gradually things began to change, and with the alterations completed in church and the three-year plan for growth in the congregation beginning to unfold, life became quite exciting. 18 months after I arrived, we welcomed as assistant curate John Willard, and he made a great contribution amongst the young people, organising all kinds of events, including a summer camp.

The Teaching Week, at the end of year two, was a course conducted by Ivor Davis, Canon Missioner of the Diocese of Southwark, a splendid teacher and strong personality. Everyone profited much from his help, and he encouraged us and helped us to be better prepared for the Parish Mission which was to follow at the end of the third year. The title of the Mission was 'Opportunity Knocks', and posters and leaflets were prepared with an attractive logo, designed by a young woman living in the parish. Leaflets were distributed all over the parish, and every week before the mission started all homes in the parish received a fresh leaflet. 'Opportunity Knocks' was painted on large banners and all kinds of preparations were made to ensure the success of the Mission. Members of the growing congregation were asked to visit every home, and attended a session of preparation and study before going out armed with notebooks, ready to make any useful comments after their sector of the parish visiting was completed.

The day of the start of 'Opportunity Knocks' arrived, and we began with a tremendous procession through the streets of the parish, led by a first rate Salvation Army band from West London and supported not only by our own members but also by clergy and people from surrounding parishes. There were special services, and special events for children, every day for eight days.

So ended our three year plan, but the end was really the beginning and everything steadily improved as we endeavoured to reap the harvest of our labours and take note of the reactions of parish visitors. Now it was time to tackle the replacement of the parish hall. There was in existence a former Army hut at the rear of the church and we needed to expand in order to provide adequate quarters for youth and other parish activities. Every Saturday evening we prepared for parish breakfast on the next day, and on Sunday mornings the growing Sunday School kindergarten also used the hall.

At this time the young ones were still singing the hymn, "Over the sea there are little brown children". We had only one coloured person in the congregation, but as the years went by, more and more coloured folk arrived. One of my extra parochial jobs was Chairman of the Borough of Wandsworth Moral and Social Welfare Committee. A small staff was employed to work in a central office. When we needed a replacement member of staff we advertised, and one applicant was from the West Indies. I asked her what job she had been doing, and she said she was employed by one of the big London firms to go backwards and forwards to the West Indies and recruit people to come over here and do various jobs which English people did not wish to do because of the unsocial hours. So it was that workers on the Underground, restaurants, domestics in hospitals and public services, came more and more from overseas.

Plans were finalised for the demolition of the old hall and the building of the new, and before too long the fresh building was up and running and enabled us to expand our parish activities. We needed the hall on Saturday evenings in order to get ready for Sunday's parish breakfast, so the policy was not to 'let' the hall on Saturdays. Several coloured folk came and wanted to hire the hall for wedding receptions and such like, but when I said the hall is not for hire on Saturdays they turned away, and I felt they were probably saying it was because of their colour we would not let it to them. Nothing could be further from the truth, but it demonstrated the difficulties we were facing when different cultures came up against each other.

The good people from the West Indies had different ideas of time keeping, and one Saturday I had to put the guests from the first wedding into the hall, to wait there until the second wedding was over, because the bride for the first wedding had still not arrived when the second wedding was due to begin! So bad was the time keeping for weddings that I ended up asking for a deposit which would be returned if they were not more than 30 minutes late. Parking for special activities was always a problem, and one day a funeral arrived very late indeed. It transpired that the address from which they had come was in the road opposite the Odeon and this was filled with cars on both sides of the road, leaving only a narrow passage in between. The funeral cortege came to pick up the family mourners, and while this was happening cars from both ends of the road met in the middle resulting in a traffic jam which became so bad the police had to be called to sort things out, hence the long, long wait at the church.

Having completed the hall we now turned our attention to tackling the unfinished part of the church building. When it was designed, the building was meant to be completed with a tower, but whether it was because the money ran out or some other reason, building work stopped, and where the tower should have been there was a long, sloping and ugly roof. So we began various money-raising activities in order to finish the building with something more beautiful and useful. What should have been the bell-ringing chamber could become a chapel and plans were made to this effect. Before long the new section of the building was completed, and we now had the Chapel of the Upper Room, with external access by a staircase from the transept door. Two sides of the chapel were fitted with glass, and so formed part of the church interior. The chapel had separate heating and was excellent for weekday services and provided a quiet haven which could be used every day for prayer and meditation.

During one Week of Prayer for Christian unity, we invited ourselves to a service in the local Roman Catholic church, in those days quite a special innovation. As a result of better relations between the churches, the Roman Catholic priest was invited to come and talk to the Deanery Synod. At the end of his address questions were asked, and one question was, "How is it that you seem able to make new converts, whereas most of our churches fail to do so?" He replied by saying that they were no better at it than anyone else, but the large influx of foreign nationals from places like Poland, where most of them were Roman Catholics, meant that they found their way to the local Roman Catholic church, settled down and had children, so naturally total numbers at the church expanded.

Every year, Billy Smart's Circus encamped on Clapham Common, and early on in our time at Balham a representative from the circus came to our door and asked if I would baptise the great granddaughter of the founder. I agreed to do so, and visited the family in their luxury caravan, and subsequently prepared them for the Baptism occasion. The service took place in the circus ring, and all the performers and the circus animals were present. Afterwards, a photograph was taken with the family and the baby in the front row, and with all the clowns and acrobats behind dressed in their performance costumes,

Star of the big top!

and at the back, the circus animals. For once in my life I became a minor celebrity, because pictures of the occasion were included in the newsreels of Pathe Gazette and shown in cinemas everywhere, and daily newspapers also included large photographs. After the baptism I was invited to the reception, asked what I would like to drink and offered a variety of alcoholic beverages. I said I would prefer just a cup of coffee, and this was met by an expression of pleasure as they said none of them drank alcohol because performing in the circus meant they had to be 100% fit, and physically and mentally alert.

As a result of this connection, each year when the circus came to town I visited them and was always presented with ringside seats for the family and myself. They explained that the children of circus families are sent to boarding school at an early age, because they are always on the move and do not stay in one place long enough for the children to be attached to a normal day school.

The Ascension vicarage had a number of rooms on the second floor which we did not use, and I suggested to the authorities that these could be turned into a self-contained flat by knocking a hole in the wall and installing an outside staircase. By doing this, the parish would have a flat for an assistant curate, and before long this came into being and Richard Love and his wife Christine moved in.

We were burgled three times during our stay in Balham. On the first occasion, during the service on Christmas Eve, the intruders knew where we were! On the second occasion we were watching the last night of the Proms. James, our youngest, had gone to bed but he re-appeared and said, "There is a funny noise in Rachel's room. I don't know if one of the cats has got shut in." Muriel went with him upstairs and suddenly the night was rent with screams. On opening Rachel's bedroom door they had come face to face with a man in a stocking mask. He pushed them out of the way, and went towards the bathroom. Hearing the screams and calls for help, I dashed upstairs and was told the man was in the bathroom, so I shut the door while telling Muriel to dial 999. Of course the intruder wasn't in the bathroom – he had climbed in that way and went out likewise. It was all very frightening and upsetting, but at least nobody was harmed. Upstairs in the flat they were recording the Prom concert, and the tape when played had all the sounds of the screams and the kerfuffle which came from below stairs.

Up to this time James was not at all nervous, but from then on would not go to bed or be left on his own, and this was so for a period of several years. We had a bed for him at the foot of ours, and then eventually he went to his own room with his door and ours left open all night. He has since recovered from this incident, but for a long time it made life difficult for him and for us.

On the third occasion we were burgled the burglar made an entry in mid afternoon and took our TV and other goods. Subsequently, the police caught up with him and found a horde of stolen goods. We were asked to go and collect everything belonging to us and so back came our TV, much to the disappointment of the children because at that time we could only get BBC1 on our set, and all new sets had BBC2. The children thought the insurance cover on the stolen set would enable us to buy a new one with access to extra channels.

Early in our stay I was appointed Honorary Canon of Southwark Cathedral, which meant I was on a rota for taking weekday Evensong and sharing in other cathedral activities. I am still invited to Cathedral 'dos', though usually I cannot manage to attend. I was also recruited as a daytime chaplain in Westminster Abbey, something I loved doing. Every hour at the Abbey the chaplain makes his way into the pulpit and asks for silence. The great multitude of visitors is stilled and a prayer for peace is said. The patron saint of the Abbey is St Peter and I was asked to preach at Evensong one Sunday on St Peter's day. It was a privilege to be doing so, and I loved the occasion and the music which went with it, and for some days after recalled the memory of it. I also preached several times at St Peter's, Eaton Square – a well-known parish church in London's West End. The vicar at that time was a fellow wartime padre, hence the connection.

Mervyn Stockwood, Bishop of Southwark, issued a three-line whip for the clergy to gather for a five-day conference at Butlin's Holiday Camp at Bognor. It was very much a new experience for most of us and one from which I benefited greatly. We stayed in the holiday chalets and shared the dining room and other facilities with holidaymakers. There were all sorts of activities for children and regular entertainments for everyone. Three bands of different calibres would play in the afternoons and evenings, and the dimensions of the buildings were such that it created a completely different world for most of the holidaymakers. Many of them came from small terraced or back-to-back homes, and the sheer scale of the buildings and the programme of activities at Butlin's was an amazing experience. No wonder Billy Butlin's enterprise was so successful.

During our stay in Balham I was asked to take a special course for the students of Dundee University and made my way by train, via Edinburgh, to Dundee. My chief memory of it is of the extreme cold. It was snowing most of the time, and I spent much of this time just trying to keep warm.

Opposite us in Balham lived a family who had relatives in the Lake District, and when they heard we wanted to go to that part of the country for our holiday they arranged for us to stay in a property which was let to holidaymakers. We thought the ideal thing would be to stay in the Lake District for a week and then move to Howarth, Brontê Country, and finally go and stay with some former parishioners now living in Macclesfield. All the plans were made and we duly arrived in the cottage in the Lake District. On arrival I noticed a large damp patch on the wall of the sitting room, but in the morning discovered that what I thought was a damp patch was actually the dry patch – the whole of the rest of the wall was damp! Everything there was very primitive and had it not been for the presence of our young family we would undoubtedly have found some other accommodation, but we stuck it out and looked forward to something better in Howarth. We could not have been more wrong in our expectations. The venue proved to be a back-to-back house with no bathroom and only a cold-water tap over an old-fashioned sink at the top of a stone staircase leading to the basement.

The lavatory was one of a block situated 50 yards down the road, and the key for it was kept on the mantelpiece, so everyone knew the object of one's journey. Imagine what it would be like in the middle of winter with a freezing north easterly wind blowing! The contrast to what we had looked forward to and what we found was so great we either had to laugh or cry, and I remember lying on the bed with Muriel beside me and seeing the funny side of it, and we laughed so much I thought the none-too-secure bed would collapse. We rang our friends in

Macclesfield and asked if we could come earlier than arranged, which we duly did. Certainly it introduced me to a style of living I had no idea still existed in Britain in the 1960's. Soon after our return from that holiday I went down with a bad attack of pneumonia and spent a great deal of September in bed.

After nine years of ups and downs in Balham I felt it was time we moved and got completely away from London for my last job, as I was already approaching 60. Quite by chance, I spotted an advertisement in the Church Times under the heading 'Exchange'. It offered a parish near the sea in the south of England, in exchange for a London benefice. The ad was under a box number and gave no idea where it was or anything about it. An exchange of benefices is perhaps a peculiar way of doing things and understandably not much welcomed by Diocesan Bishops, as it denies them any part in the choice of the best man for a job, though the Bishop does have to signify he has no objection. No harm in applying and finding out more, I thought, so I did, and soon received a letter saying the writer had received several letters besides mine, but would like to check with my request first.

Country Ways

The upshot was an expedition to the benefice of Blendworth, Chalton and Idsworth in Hampshire – parts of it in lovely countryside and about 10 miles form the sea. The rector took me round to see the churches: one, at Blendworth, was Victorian and the other two were very ancient buildings, the one at Idsworth having some 14th century wall paintings. The rectory was lovely in every respect, set in a garden, quite large but not too large for management. All the rooms in the house face south, and from the bedrooms, on a clear day, it is possible to see the sea. Everything about it was in absolute contrast to life in London, the house, the garden, the churches, the countryside, all calling out to me, and under my breath I found myself saying, "I'll never be lucky enough to get it".

I was more than happy at the prospect of the move, but the Rector of Blendworth had to come to London to inspect the church, the home and the parish at Balham to see if this was the type of place he wished to serve and before any concrete proposal on our exchange could be considered and the necessary steps put in motion to bring it about. Why did he want to move? Because he and his wife found they did not enjoy country life, and the situation at Blendworth, Chalton and Idsworth in the Hampshire countryside. So he came to London and visited the Ascension, Balham. After he had returned home I had to sit back and wait for his decision. To move or not to move, that was the question. A few days later a letter arrived saying he would be happy to come to Balham, so both of us could approach our Diocesan Bishops and make arrangements for the exchange to proceed.

We were excited and full of joyful expectation as the necessary legal business took place, and the institution at Blendworth was fixed for November 1970. The day came for our removal, giving each of us time beforehand to arrange for things like curtains and carpets and to give us a period of three weeks before starting duty. So we were at the beginning of a new life, and some of my friends and former parishioners went to spy out the land and thought I had taken leave of my senses in moving to this very different area. I had always served in large, heavily populated parishes in the London district, but I had not acted without much thought and prayer. My family roots were bound up with the countryside and for my last job I wanted a complete change of environment.

Within a short period I realised people are the same wherever they live. The environment changes, but the people very little. As I went about the parish and settled into our new home, my heart sang, visiting farms and cottages in place of rows of houses and blocks of flats, and driving along country lanes instead of busy highways. The garden gave me much scope for exercise and I loved it all, as well as appreciating the delightful house. My brother in law, also a priest, thought the rectory one of the best in the country.

Within a short period of time in our new home we had the services of a former estate worker assisting us in the garden. He came for only four hours a week, but what he did was worth its weight in gold. We had a fruit cage with all kinds of soft fruit, and there were apple and pear trees. Mr Creswell prepared the ground for a kitchen garden and planted every kind of vegetable, all grown from his own plants in a small greenhouse in his back garden. He more than repaid our outgoings, and later on when I said I felt I should pay him more but I regretted that it was all I could afford, he just looked at me and said, "If I didn't like it, I wouldn't come".

Holy Trinity, Blendworth

The day of the institution at Blendworth arrived and the telephone rang and an angry voice said, "Are you the Rector?" I replied that I supposed I was but that I had only just arrived. Apparently the good lady was on the flower rota for the following Sunday at Idsworth and went to do the flowers only to find they were already done. There wasn't much I could do about it, but in fact what had happened was that the lady doing the flowers the previous Sunday had provided some lovely chrysanthemums and being left in a cold church they gave the appearance of fresh flowers. The irate voice on the phone made me turn to Muriel and say, "You're welcome".

If this was not enough, I went into the church and found no cross or candlesticks on the altar. I presumed someone had taken them away to clean them for the special occasion that evening. In fact, someone had taken them away but not to clean! They were never recovered and had to be replaced. So, not altogether a good start in my new parish. Within days the telephone rang to tell me the church of St Hubert's Idsworth was on fire. The fire had been spotted from the window of a neighbouring house and the fire brigade were already tackling the blaze when I arrived at the scene. Fortunately the fire had not taken complete hold and only the vestry and part of the chancel were destroyed. This unique building, many centuries old, would never have been rebuilt had the fire really gained a hold. A new vestry was built and repairs carried out, though it is still possible to find various scars left by pieces of the burning roof falling down.

So, first the altar flowers, second the cross and candlesticks, third the fire, but even this was not enough. I visited Chalton Church soon after and parked my car on the slope outside the church, went in to collect something and returned to see the car, with Muriel inside it, careering down the hill. The handbrake cable had broken, but fortunately some men working on a cottage nearby spotted what had happened and managed to bring the car to a stop against the hedge before it went completely out of control. Moral: never rely on a handbrake – always leave it in gear!

That was the way things began during the first two months, and then I underwent an operation for gallstones in Westminster Hospital. All was going well and I was due to return home, but suffered an embolism on my lung and as a consequence was somewhat unwell and kept in hospital. Afterwards, Muriel and I went to stay with her brother and his wife. He was a farm manager at Godstone in Surrey. Eventually we were back in our new home at Blendworth and with some hope of really getting down to work in our new parish. Not yet though, because after 10 days I had another embolism and was admitted to St Mary's Hospital in Portsmouth. More weeks went by, and what the parishioners thought of their new incumbent I cannot imagine. Certainly events seemed to conspire against my advent. When the time came for my retirement, 11 years later, one of the churchwardens at the farewell said they had wondered if I would last 11 weeks, let alone 11 years.

Eventually I did get going after this rather disastrous beginning: Blendworth Church is a pleasant Victorian building, and it replaced the original village church of St Giles, half a mile down the lane. The name survives at St Giles Farm, opposite the site of the old church. St Giles had proved much too small for the expanding village of Horndean, and after Gales Brewery was established in the village, cottages were built for the workers and a new and larger church of the Holy Trinity was erected. In its turn this building also became too small, and while I was there we had the problem of increasing the seating accommodation. On occasions the church was too full for comfort and safety and various ideas were considered, such as extending the west wall or building a gallery, but the cost of either was enormous and in the end we put flaps on the ends of the pews and the choir stalls.

What exactly happened to bring about the demolition of the ancient village church of St Giles I never discovered. All that was left was the churchyard wall, broken gravestones and the original foundations. Half the members of the PCC did not even know the old churchyard existed, and as far as the local population was concerned, over the wall went all manner of rubbish and unwanted goods – old bedsteads and furniture, old bicycles, in fact it was an ideal rubbish dump enclosed by the old stone churchyard wall. This presented me with a problem. Surely it was not right that the site of the old church and burial ground be left derelict in this way, so we organised a working party every Saturday afternoon which continued for many months. First we shifted the mountains of rubbish, then dug out brambles and elder and other unwanted growth, and finally marked out the lines of the foundations of the old church with pieces of gravestones. We were then given the gift of turf and the whole area was turfed over and a seat provided so as to create a garden of remembrance.

It seemed that as long as the ruins of the church and churchyard lay forgotten under mountains of rubbish and completely overgrown, nobody seemed to mind, and presumably it would have gone on like that forever. But a soon as I organised working parties to restore it, all manner of officials began to take an interest and tell me what I could and couldn't do. Moral: do nothing and all is well. Do something, and everyone will tell you how to do it and complain it should have been done before! Many good folk worked really hard to restore the site and we owe a great debt to them for all the hard labour involved.

Chalton was once a flourishing village with its own rector and assistant curate who looked after Idsworth Church as well. There is a memorial in the sanctuary which gives a delightful testimonial for a really faithful parish priest of long ago. The village, when I arrived, still had its own shop and post office, but before long they were closed and villagers now have to travel quite a few miles to the nearest post office and stores. Such is the way of things today. Everyone is urged to be 'green', and use public transport, but villagers in places like Chalton have no means of getting anywhere except by using a car. Inside the church, we restored the organ and carried out various improvements which means the church now looks clean, lovely and well cared for. The churchwarden when we arrived was Griff Kewley, and as I write he is still there but is now churchwarden-emeritus. Largely because of all he has done, and inspired others to do, he has now become a Lay Canon of Portsmouth Cathedral – a well-deserved honour. Without him the church would surely have been declared redundant.

Idsworth is one of the smallest churches in the kingdom and started life as a hunting chapel. Among important items of furniture it has 14th century wall paintings and a small organ in the gallery. Derek Hickman was organist when we came, and 38 years later he still is. He has the capacity of making quite a small instrument sound like something much larger, and has done, and still is doing, wonderful service. Another remarkable thing, and certainly original, is the large stone plinth at the entrance to the path leading up the hill to the church. The stone was brought all the way from a quarry in the west country, and bears the details of the name of the church and its services. This was erected instead of having this ancient church display details of services on a painted wooden board, and it remains a permanent memorial to the initiative of John Edney and his helpers.

There are then three churches in the benefice: Holy Trinity Blendworth, St Michael and All Angels Chalton, and St Hubert Idsworth, There is no actual village of Idsworth and it is said that it was wiped out during the Black Death, but there is still Idsworth House and the site of a village school. When the railway came, the owners of the manor house would not accept the railway running at the foot of their drive and so a replacement Idsworth

House was built on its present site, a mile or so away. An avenue of trees running up the hillside to where the original house once stood can still be seen.

Having three churches to care for meant planning a system enabling the rector to be, as it were, in three places at once! Every Sunday at Blendworth there was an 8.00 a.m and an 11.00 a.m and a service at Idsworth at 10.00 a.m. This latter service meant I had to run down the hill afterwards and speed through the lanes to get to Blendworth by 11.00. I used to say that I gave out the first hymn at Blendworth in the same breath as I gave out the last one at Idsworth. On one Sunday in the month there was a Sung Eucharist held at Chalton, and I had to get someone to take the service at Idsworth in order to be at Chalton. On the first Sunday in every month the choir and congregation of Blendworth joined the congregation at Chalton for Evensong. Nowadays it is not at all unusual for incumbents to have more than one church, but the drawback is that rushing from one to the other gives no opportunity for staying behind after the service and fraternising. At Blendworth, after the morning service most of the congregation came over to the rectory for coffee etc, and in the summer everyone enjoyed the delights of the rectory garden.

There were two Church schools in the neighbourhood, at Blendworth and at Horndean. The first named was built next to the church and was very much a village school. Alas it is no more, being deemed too small and too expensive in today's scheme of things. Every Wednesday morning the children from Blendworth came into church for their assembly. There is also a large church school down the hill in Horndean and I took the assembly there every Thursday morning. Horndean has grown into quite a large housing area, but it has no parish church, the area being served by Blendworth on the south side and Catherington on the north.

The parish hall (called the Nash Hall after a beloved local doctor) was situated in a most awkward position right on the corner of the main Portsmouth Road, and a steady stream of traffic went past and drowned out the voice of any speaker inside the hall. It also meant that the exit was directly adjacent to a very busy highway. A few years later the A3(M) was built to alleviate the traffic problem, but even so the road remains very busy. All things considered I thought the hall very unworkable, so first of all I asked Andrew, my son who is an architect, to suggest ways of improving it, but then I realised we were wasting our time and any money spent on it. What was needed was a new hall on an adjacent site. But where could this be?

I identified some land where I thought a new church centre could be built to meet the needs of Blendworth and Horndean. So after spying out the land I went to the owners and asked if we could have the corner of the field at the bottom of Blendworth Hill. The Murray family, who lived at Cadlington House, held a family conclave at which I was present, and asked me what my ideas were and what would happen after I was no longer rector. Fortunately, I was able to satisfy any misgivings they had and they agreed to give the land to us, so I was able to take the next step and consult the PCC. Then we held a public meeting to outline future plans. The idea was to build not just a hall but a church centre which would incorporate a chapel for weekday services, a small hall adjacent to the large hall, both with easy access to a modern kitchen, and the large hall would have sliding doors across it, so that it could be used for activities not needing the entire space. No stage was planned: instead, stage blocks would be on site and these could be moved into whatever position most suitable for any proposed event.

At the public meeting, and after much discussion, it was generally agreed the plan should go ahead – but not without some gloomy expressions of opinion. Some said it would never be built, and others said it might, but not in their lifetime. An architect was chosen, plans submitted and the project costed. The next problem was how to pay for it.

The Nash Hall was adjacent to buildings belonging to Gales Brewery, and we offered to sell our premises to them. Fortunately they were delighted to purchase them at a time when we wished to vacate the building. So we were well on the way, and started all sorts of fundraising activities, everyone working with a will. In 12 months, the foundation stone of the new building was laid, and one year later the Bishop of Portsmouth dedicated the new Blendworth and Horndean Church Centre. In just another 12 months we were completely free of debt, and the parish had a splendid church centre, enabling us to expand and develop many parish activities.

At the annual general meeting held after the opening, I said in my remarks that the parish had worked so hard in so many ways, we should rest a while before discussing further plans. Immediately a member jumped up and said, "We don't need a rest. We all enjoyed the project and I propose we build new vestries." I asked if this was a proper proposal, and if so it would need a seconder before being put to the meeting. A seconder was forthcoming at once and so it was put to the meeting. Only one hand was raised against and that was by my son James. Afterwards I asked him why, and he said because he thought I didn't really want it!

The church at Blendworth had only a tiny clergy vestry, so small that wedding couples and their families could not get into it together and had to wait in the church for the signing of the register and file in as needed. The choir vestry was altogether too small for the number in the choir and there was no water supply. So plans were made to build a larger choir vestry with cupboard space designed to assist flower arrangers, and the clergy vestry doubled in size with a washbasin etc.

The new buildings were duly completed and the outside constructed in stone, matching the east end of the church. Nowadays it has mellowed, and it is hard to believe the new addition is a mere 40 years old. In every parish I worked in I had a great deal to do with builders. First in Lambeth, repairing war damage. Second, at Surbiton, building a new hall and new choir vestry and toilet facilities. At Balham, another new hall and the completion of the church building, and now at Blendworth the church centre and new vestries etc. So surely, I say to myself, I will go down in history as a builder. My only hope is that it is not only as a builder concerned with bricks and mortar but also with building congregations.

Parking at Blendworth was always a problem, and one Sunday morning the police came into church during the service because the local fire engine from the station at the bottom of the hill could not get past the cars parked outside. What were we to do about this increasing problem? It so happened that the farm opposite the rectory was put up for sale and the owner had decided to sell it in plots rather than as a whole, so we went ahead to see if we could obtain the corner field alongside the east end of the church and opposite the rectory. This would create a large parking place, and also provide a playing field which could be used both by the school and by our young people for church activities. The education authorities were called in and were persuaded that there was a real need for a school playing field. So all obstacles were overcome and the field and the car park came into our possession and have proved a great blessing.

On my arrival at my first ever country parish, when Rogation Sunday came round I asked if anything was done to mark it. I could hardly believe the answer was 'no'. So I went round to farmers in the district and asked them to send a tractor and trailer on Rogation Sunday. The plan was to hold a short service in church, and then set off to cover the area of the parishes and hold a short service in each village and other strategic points - at Chalton, for example, opposite the Red Lion (one of the oldest inns in Hampshire) many people mill would around outside on a Sunday evening. One tractor and trailer would take the choir; another would transport the Westbourne Salvation Army band; other tractors and trailers would carry the rest of the congregation and people could also travel in private cars. On return, refreshments would be served at the rectory.

On the next Rogation Sunday, and thereafter, tractors and trailers arrived in the early evening, and after a short service in church everyone climbed on board and off we went, stopping for prayers for farmers and for a blessing on growing crops and giving thanks for all the gifts of God's creation. The procession grew in numbers as the years went by and we were joined by congregations from other churches, notably the people from St Philip's Cosham, and their young vicar Peter Price, who is now

Bishop of Bath and Wells. It seemed the Rogation procession would carry on in the same way for always, but now, because of insurance and safety regulations, tractors and trailers are no longer forthcoming, and instead the procession is a parish walk followed by a barbecue.

Work with young people was, and is, a priority and young Sunday School teachers were doing wonderful things in the Church School. We gathered a few youngsters together on a Friday evening after choir practice in the dining room at the Rectory, and formed what became known as the 'Friday Knights'. Before going home, one of the young people would lead us in prayers and all of us would sing the hymn 'When the Knights of old". The dining room eventually became too small for our growing numbers and we used the Nash Hall until the new church centre was built. The Friday Knights became well known in the district, and they served at the tables at the harvest supper and played a prominent part in the life of the three parishes.

One day the telephone rang and a lady living in the parish told me she went in for all sorts of competitions and over the years had won quite a few, and now she had a claim on a minibus. In order to get it, however, she had to say how it would be used, and so she was asking me if we had such a thing what we would do with it. Once I had recovered from my surprise and excitement, I said the Friday Knights would be delighted to have the use of it and we would provide a Sunday morning bus service to bring old and disabled people to church. The donors of the minibus were satisfied the bus would be put to good use and made arrangements for a special presentation to hand it over to us in Portsmouth. So we took back to Blendworth a brand new minibus with "The Friday

Knights" painted in bold letters on both sides, and thereafter the Sunday morning bus service was organised.

The Friday Knights grew in number, and I decided we needed a leader other than myself and asked Janet Laws, who ran the Sunday School, if she would take it on. She did so, and did wonderful work in the following years. She took the bus and the Friday Knights for weekends at Youth Hostels, and in the summer to the seaside, and generally gave herself totally in serving the young people and the parish. We were much blessed in having her. It is good to say that at the time of writing she is secretary to the Bishop of London and happily serving the church in that position.

Relations with our local Roman Catholic Church in Horndean were good, and the parish priest, Michael, quite often came to the rectory for a chat, and he asked me to preach in the Roman Catholic Church. The Roman Catholics came to our Lent lunches, and took their turn in serving them. When Michael was moved elsewhere, his successor arrived and I thought I should call on him and welcome him and introduce myself. I went to the presbytery, to be greeted at the front door with "What do you want?" I said I did not want anything but I was rector of Blendworth, Chalton and Idsworth and came to make myself known and to welcome him. He said, "If you wish to speak to me you must make an appointment." And that was that. I was glad many of his parishioners were upset when they heard about it and they continued to come and play their part in serving the Lent lunches at the church centre.

Apart from normal routine parish work I continued to carry out various other duties, and soon after my arrival at Blendworth the bishop asked me to care for older men who were interested in training for the Sacred Ministry. The idea was for me to run a study group for potential candidates, and they would be asked to read designated books, write essays, and discuss general theological topics. I agreed to do as the bishop asked, and an interesting number and variety of men came my way. One of them already had a doctorate degree and was very knowledgeable. One essay he handed to me I found hard to mark because it was so good. I sent it to Salisbury Theological College, under whose auspices we were working, and asked them for comments. It came back marked A+ (or almost perfect). At that time the Southern Diocesan Ministry Training Scheme had not been formed, and I attended meetings which resulted in there being no further need for me to see men at home because a proper training scheme came into being.

The bishop also asked me to take the Ordination Retreat and preach at the Ordination service. The retreat was at Catherington House, the then Diocesan Retreat and Conference Centre, and the ordination at St Mary, Portsea. Altogether an exciting and rather humbling experience. St Mary Portsea is an extremely large parish church, well known as a training centre for curates, many of whom eventually held high office as bishops or even archbishops. Later on I took another retreat and preached at the ordination service in Portsmouth Cathedral.

The years went swiftly and happily by, and I was now approaching my 70th birthday and wondering where and how we could find a new home for our retirement. At that time there was no provision of housing for retired clergy in the manner the Pensions Board now provide it. Sir Lynton White, who was patron of the living at Blendworth, Chalton and Idsworth, asked me where I was going to live when I retired, and I told him I had no idea, whereupon he said, "Would my aunt's bungalow do?" His aunt, Pauline White, was well known to me as a member of the congregation at Idsworth Church and I had visited her on many occasions. She had become increasingly infirm and had to leave her home and enter a nursing home. The bungalow, in Rowlands Castle, was offered to us at a generously low rent, and I accepted the offer with joy and alacrity. The house was just about perfect for retirement. Besides the main part of the house there is an annexe with its own bathroom etc, just ideal for family and other visitors to come and stay.

Retirement

So in October 1981, after 11 years as Rector of Blendworth, Chalton and Idsworth, we bade farewell, and after a splendid send off moved into the bungalow. The years in the last of my places of service were very happy and we received much generous support and made many friends, and now we were extremely fortunate in having the opportunity to live in the attractive house at Rowlands Castle. The garden was rather smaller than we had had before but just about right for my own gardening efforts, something I have always much enjoyed.

Now came the question of where we should worship. The obvious thing would be to attend the local parish church, but when I left Blendworth the Diocesan Authorities decided to do some regrouping of parishes and Rowlands Castle was linked with Blendworth, Chalton and Idsworth. This meant I would not really be leaving the parish at all, if we worshipped there, and I felt this was not an ideal situation. I had to help people to love my successor and forget all about me, so we decided we would attend the mid-week service at Rowlands Castle but find a new spiritual home somewhere else. We attended the Cathedral and various churches in the area, one of which was St John's, Westbourne, and here we felt it was just right for us. The friendliness of the people and our welcome, plus the beauty of the church, added up to our decision to join the congregation. Thus began an attachment that lasted over 25 years.

The word went round that I had retired and almost straight away I was asked to fill in at other churches covering holidays and where clergy were in short supply. I accepted most invitations and did duty in 33 different churches in the nearby district. An interesting experience for me, though I must admit on occasions it was somewhat depressing. In one church the pace of the hymns was so slow I had to look round and see if the organist was still there because the breaks between the verses were so long, and even worse was the pace of the hymn itself!

Westbourne became a much-loved centre for our devotions and the source of many friendships and happy occasions. Peter Baden was rector at this time, and in my first year asked me to take a quiet day for the PCC, a Lent course and conduct the Three Hours on Good Friday. Then at the start of the second year he telephoned and said he had accepted another living and would be leaving quite soon, so would I look after the parish during the interregnum? Westbourne was grouped with Forestside, Stansted and Woodmancote – four churches in all, and the parish magazine was called 'Four'. Forestside had a part time priest who lived at Forestside and he assisted the rector. Later it was decided an assistant priest would be more useful if attached to Compton and the Marden group of churches, leaving Westbourne and Woodmancote together.

I quite happily agreed to do duty after Peter Baden left for as long as the interregnum lasted, expecting it to be for a period of three or four months and certainly not anticipating any difficulty in filling the vacancy because Westbourne is an attractive place in which to work. The rectory and parish hall are both opposite the church and set in a village with all necessary amenities. The church had, and still has, a fine team of bellringers, splendid choir and organ and a fine musical tradition. Altogether an attractive prospect, and had I been 10 years younger I would have jumped at the chance of becoming the rector.

The interregnum I expected to last a short while became altogether a different experience from what could have been forecast. The normal procedure for filling the vacancy was followed, and a new man appointed, and expected to start at the beginning of July, but at the last moment he decided not to come. He had a severely handicapped child and his plan was to move the child to a Home nearer to Westbourne, but at this late stage he and his wife decided it was not fair on the child and they must leave him where he was happy and well cared for. So we were back in square one and had to begin the process of appointing a new man all over again. July and August are two months of the year when it seems everyone is on holiday and it is difficult to get in touch with anyone. So this took us to September when Muriel and I went away for a pre-arranged holiday.

On our return the telephone rang and Freda Laws, one of the churchwardens, said, "I'm afraid I have some bad news for you." She then told me we had squatters in the rectory. My instinct was to get together some strong men and go and throw them out, but I was informed we could not do so. If premises have been vacant for six months or more, such a thing as Squatters' Rights come into play, and what we had to do was prove our need for the house and get a Court order to eject the intruders.

Accordingly we applied and got the necessary order and the squatters were given notice to quit in November. Meanwhile the parish treated them very kindly and gave them gifts of harvest produce etc. The day after the squatters moved out, the churchwardens and I went to inspect the inside of the building and found it had been just about totally destroyed. Heaps of rubbish everywhere, smashed fittings and holes in the ceiling so that standing on the ground floor one could see the sky. Of course the police were informed and the culprits taken to court and dealt with, but what it meant to the parish was - no rectory, so no rector!

The diocese had then to decide what to do about restoring the house, and after much discussion, with people divided 'for' and 'against', it was decided it would cost thousands of pounds to make the house serviceable again and modernise it, so it would be better to sell the remains plus part of the garden, and then build a new rectory in the rest of the garden. What to do meanwhile? When a suitable house became available in the village and near the church, the diocese bought it, so at last a new incumbent was possible, and eventually Kenneth Grace was appointed. All this palaver took just about two years, so by the time of the institution of the new rector I had to all intents and purposes been rector of Westbourne for two years. During this time I had come to know the people and the village and felt part and parcel of the set up. In later years I would take two more interregnums at Westbourne.

Nearing the end

Retirement was, for me, a kind of new beginning and surpassed anything I could have hoped for. We had, of course, no idea of our future, and I was decidedly fortunate in that I kept physically fit and had the opportunity of continuing my ministry. I owe much to successive rectors for their kindness in allowing me to play my part. When Kenneth Grace retired we had the all too short stay of Brian Marshall, and then began the faithful ministry of Richard Wells. After 11 years he is still working at Westbourne and carrying on the good work.

Being able to worship and work at Westbourne was a great bonus and made retirement much more fulfilling than anyone could possibly have imagined. We were able to indulge ourselves by taking holidays of a kind not dreamed of, no longer constrained by parish work and lack of money. We planned a tour of Canada and America visiting former friends and neighbours, and some of our cousins now living in Toronto. As a result of a generous leaving present from Blendworth, Chalton and Idsworth we had the necessary wherewithal, and because retirement places no restriction on the timetable we could now put into action plans for the kind of holiday we never thought possible.

We wrote to our contacts in all the different places we planned to visit and fixed up dates to cover all our movements, and all was arranged in terms of staging points and times and days. I went to Thomas Cook in Chichester and asked them to finalise our travel arrangements in such a manner that all I had to do was pay the bill in Chichester and then collect from them flight tickets, train tickets, Greyhound Bus tickets, sea passage tickets to Victoria Island and a voucher for a one night's stay in a hotel in Vancouver.

The necessary arrangements made for us by Thomas Cook were quite splendid. We were about to travel across the Atlantic to Canada, and then right across that country and the length of the United States, from Vancouver to San Francisco and to Tucson on the Mexican border and all I had to do was pack our bags and take a folder of papers and dole out the necessary vouchers as we made our progress.

On Thursday May 20th we left London airport and duly boarded our plane, which was Air Canada, and after an extremely smooth flight landed in Halifax, Nova Scotia. We were met at the airport by Sue and Roger Buxton who drove us to their house at Bedford about 20 miles away. The Buxtons were our next-door neighbours at Blendworth for two years, and they had been back and stayed with us on two or three occasions. This was our first sight of Canada and it seemed impossible to believe we were on the other side of the Atlantic Ocean and had been in England just a few hours before.

Psalm 72, "His dominion shall be from one sea to the other, and from the flood unto the world's end". Canada is always known as 'The Dominion of Canada' because geographically it almost entirely fits the description contained in Psalm 72. On the east coast, the Atlantic Ocean, on the west coast, the Pacific Ocean, to the south, the great lakes forming the United States of America border, and to the north, the far Arctic region. So 'The Dominion of Canada is from sea to sea and from the lakes unto the world's end'.

On our first day we went round the city of Halifax,

which is quite a busy centre with its university and cathedral, and then along the coast to various points and coves and had a picnic lunch by the waterside. The weather had been sunny ever since our arrival, but with rather a cold wind. This is the east coast of Canada, and like the east coast of England it is often quite chilly in the spring. In the evening we watched the cup final on television, a very strange thing to find it being shown on Canadian TV. Next day, Sunday, we went to the church of St Peter at Birch Cove nearby, which is the church Sue and Roger attend. The service was parish communion and the church quite full, and we were told it is normally well attended. The order of service was according to the Canadian Book of Common Prayer and very similar to our own prayer book at home.

The previous Sunday evening, in 'Songs of Praise' on BBC TV Tony Galvin, one of the Tottenham Hotspur players, was interviewed and chose as his favourite hymn 'Let Us Break Bread Together'. The day before on the television I had been watching him play at Wembley, and then this morning the hymn at the communion in church was 'Let Us Break Bread Together', an enjoyable coincidence. That afternoon we went for a walk and in the evening set off for Halifax to attend an ordination service at the Cathedral of All Saints. This was an interesting experience in every way, the service, the choir, and the music, everything just as if it had been picked up and dropped on the other side of the ocean. I have always been conscious of belonging to the worldwide church, and somehow this made it seem particularly real. The Archbishop of Cape Town, South Africa was present and gave the blessing, so from different parts of the world we were sharing in it together.

Next day was observed in Canada as a public holiday, a custom dating back to our old Empire Day May 24th, long since forgotten at home except by a few oldies. Everything on this side of the world was looking rather beautiful and fresh green as we visited the oldest Church of England church in Canada, St Paul's Halifax. Not really very old as far as we're concerned. Everything over there is old if it's a hundred or so years old. When we returned in the evening we were able to watch the replay of the cup final. How extraordinary our modern world is, here I was sitting in an armchair 3,000 miles away from home in Canada watching Tottenham win the cup at Wembley.

One of the interesting things about our stay in Halifax was the fact that pedestrians have the right of way when crossing the road. If motorists saw you wanted to cross they stopped. We felt we could certainly take a leaf out of Canadian books in this respect, and we also found everyone very friendly and polite.

The following Sunday was Whit Sunday and that morning I preached and assisted at the Parish Communion at St Peter's, Birch Grove. The order of service was much like our own Series 3, and everyone was very warm in their welcome, the rector especially so. Quite an experience to be involved in the service in this way, and we found it hard to believe we were so very far away from home. Two of the Buxton's neighbours, who are Roman Catholics, came to church with us that morning and made their communion with the approval of their own parish priest. That evening we went to Halifax for Evensong in the Cathedral, and again everything was exactly as if we had been present in one of our own English cathedrals.

Next morning we left by plane for Toronto where we

were met at the Airport by Linda and Philip Voo, two former parishioners from the Ascension, Balham, whose wedding ceremony I had performed some 17 years ago, and they had come out here about 14 years ago. They drove us to their home at Orangeville, which is a small town outside Toronto. It is much cooler in this part of the world than where we had been before, and we had heavy rain in the night before setting off at 10 in the morning to explore Toronto. The centre of that City is very impressive with its wonderful shopping centre - the best we've ever seen - and masses and masses of goods for sale though almost everything struck us as being expensive. We went to the railway station to make sure all was well for our great train journey which was due to begin in two or three days time. The station was most impressive, and we've never seen one so good, spacious, clean and well organised. British Rail could learn a thing or two! On the way back to Toronto and Orangeville we stopped and had supper. People eat out much more over there than is the case in England, and we found the prices very cheap in comparison and the food very good.

Next day we visited Black Creek Village just outside Toronto, which has a collection of buildings, workshops, farms, etc all from the very early stages of the settlers in Canada, giving one some idea of what it must have been like when they first came and explored this vast country. In the afternoon we visited my cousin Fred and his wife Eleanor. My mother's sister emigrated with her husband in 1906 and Fred is her son. Fred and his wife have been to England two or three times and have stayed at Blendworth, so we were not strangers. They were especially delighted to see us because we were the very first of the family ever to make their way across the ocean to their home in

Toronto.

While we were in Orangeville we were taken by Linda to have a look at their parish church and everything there. The church itself was very nice with marvellous facilities, 'on the spot' rooms for meetings, Sunday School, cloakrooms, hall, rector's office, secretary's office and so on and so on., which is a great advantage. Most of our own churches in England virtually have no facilities at all, or if they have they are often not on the same scale and extremely cramped. This small town had several good shopping centres, libraries and other public services.

We were enjoying our stay, travelling all over the place and being shown all sorts of interesting things, for example being taken to the Chinese quarter. Philip and Linda are Chinese in origin, and we had the most amazing Chinese meal. That same evening we ended up at Toronto station and boarded the famous Canadian Pacific train bound for Vancouver. We were shown to our cabin, which had two wide and comfortable bunk beds and with our own washing facilities. So to bed, for our first night on the train. We'd been warned beforehand that whatever we did we must book first class, and there's no doubt it was the right thing to do, because we had our own cabin with facilities, whereas second class passengers merely had a curtain round bunks in the main part of the train and shared washing facilities.

Next day was Trinity Sunday. We hadn't slept too well, and it seemed more than a little strange to be getting up and facing several days and nights on a train, yet here we were, and enjoyed our breakfast in a most comfortable dining car, and then explored the train, found the observation car, the buffet car and so on. On returning to our cabin we found the beds had 'disappeared', and in their place we had two very comfortable armchairs - all very clever. One of the beds had gone up into the ceiling and the other into the wall, and on this Sunday morning we said Matins together and Ante-Communion, and remembered especially where we lived and the congregation at Blendworth.

The views from the train of the lakes and trees were beautiful, just as we imagined they would be. The hours went by very quickly, gazing, reading, wandering up and down the train, enjoying our meals and so on. We got off the train at several places for a few moments, at stations with wonderful sounding names - for example: Thunder Bay, Medicine Hat, Moose Jaw, Indian Head and Swift Current. When the train stopped at a station it was really like a bus stop, with no platform or anything, and one just gets off and wanders away. No one seemed the least bit concerned about tickets. We spent many hours in the observation car enjoying the scenery of the lakes and mountains. The train goes all along the edge of Lake Superior, and it was a lovely day and lovely evening, just ideal for such a journey.

The train went meandering along, threading its way like a snake, all 18 coaches of it. It twisted and turned this way and that, never going very fast, and Muriel said it completely exceeded all her expectations. Next day it was raining again. I don't think anybody can say it's only in England we get bad weather. We had been away from England for three weeks and the weather couldn't have been more like the English climate if we'd especially ordered it.

That day we crossed the vast open spaces of the Prairies and had a train stop at Winnipeg for 3 ½ hours, so we were able to get off and go sightseeing. We took a real ex-London red double-decker bus on a tour. Soon the train was taking us through the Rocky Mountains and on to Calgary, a city we didn't particularly like because it has been over commercialised, but we had hour after hour after hour of breathtaking scenery as the train almost literally crawled round hairpin bends and in and out of tunnels. The railway line is a marvellous feat of engineering and this trip we were on is one that many people dream about and never have the chance to enjoy.

On arrival at Vancouver Station we took a taxi to the bus station and from there went by bus to the ferry en route for Victoria, British Columbia. We expected this journey on the ferry to be quite short, but it is a 20-mile journey, and we were able to see quite a bit of Vancouver and its environs. The ferry to Vancouver Island takes about 1½ hours, and it was a marvellous journey with lovely views of the islands, and snow capped mountains in the distance. It was an unexpected bonus because we hadn't expected anything like this sea journey through such lovely scenery.

On arrival at Vancouver Island we had another 20-mile journey to the home of Jane and Robin Knapp-Fisher in Victoria. They were living at Church Cottage in Blendworth when we arrived there in 1970, and they met us at the bus station here and took us to their very nice home. In the afternoon we went sightseeing, and in the evening were taken out to dinner to a restaurant with a breathtaking view of the sea and the mountains, and then finished the day down at the harbour and walked round watching the glorious sunset over the mountains and sea. When it got dark all the buildings were floodlit and it was like fairyland. Victoria is lovely and this is the nicest part of Canada that we visited.

Next day was a lovely day and we took it easy in the morning, bought postcards to send back to people in England and sat in the garden reading and writing. We decided we wouldn't mind living in this part of the world, and there haven't been many places that we have visited which we would have swapped for England's green and pleasant land. After a quick lunch in the garden we left for a lovely, drive to the Boutchart gardens. These are beautiful beyond words, a riot of colour, trees, flowers and plants in an incredible setting. Of all the gardens we have ever visited, I would rank these as number one - quite delightful. We were blessed with a perfect day, blue sky and a temperature of 80 degrees but with a lovely fresh breeze so it didn't feel in the least bit too warm, and we returned home to a supper of locally caught halibut. So ended our wonderful day.

The time came for us to leave Victoria Island on the ferry back to Vancouver, but before we returned we visited a museum. Not that we are very keen on museums, but this museum is described as a 'must'. It records many examples of the first colonisation of British Columbia and shows in a very vivid way the incredible trials and tribulations of our ancestors some 250 years ago. It also shows how we have destroyed Indian culture. We have much to answer for in this way. We thoroughly enjoyed our visit to the museum and took leave of the Knapp-Fishers after a marvellous few days. The sea journey is about the same as if crossing the English Channel though on the map it looked as if Vancouver to Victoria was just across a river.

I have mentioned this delightful journey and on that day it was particularly beautiful. On our arrival in Vancouver we made our way to our hotel, the only hotel we stayed in during the six weeks of our holiday. We were given a key to a most fantastic suite with bedroom, large sitting room, bathroom, television and a balcony, which was extraordinary, and so good we thought there must be some mistake. However we unpacked and enjoyed it, and wished we could have invited all our friends to come and enjoy it with us. 28 floors up, and the views from the windows were quite incredible - the whole city of Vancouver spread out below, and when it got dark all the lights below looked like fairyland.

In the morning we went by taxi to the bus station to board a Greyhound Bus to take us to San Francisco. The bus system goes just about everywhere, and there are stops on the way for cloakrooms, restaurants and so on. Our journey would take just about 24 hours, and we chose this way of travel in order to see as much of America as possible. We went round Seattle, Eugene and other American towns, but the countryside was very ordinary and nothing to write home about. Our journey on the Greyhound bus was much over-rated and an experience I wouldn't recommend for a long journey.

We arrived at Oakland, just outside San Francisco, at 7.30 in the morning and were met by Frank Wootton, a friend of the family, who drove us to his home at Walnut Creek. There we met Virginia, his wife, and after a wash and brush up and a change of clothing were ready to start the day and left on a sightseeing tour. We were shown round the sights of San Francisco which we found outstanding in every way, wonderful bridges, mountains and the sea and although we were very tired when we reached home it was an experience we shall never forget.

We had a wonderful few days in San Francisco, looking round the town, enjoying ourselves, and it was wonderful to watch the world go by. All the big hotels seem to make a point of allowing anyone to use the lifts, which are on the outside of the buildings and go up some 30 storeys or so, and one can have a good look round at the top. We also made our way to Grace Cathedral, the Anglican Cathedral of the Diocese of California, and were just in time to join in a celebration of Holy Communion. The notice board informed us that Evensong was being sung by the cathedral choir at 5.15, for all the world as if were back home in one of our own English cathedrals instead of being some 7 or 8 thousand miles away.

When we returned we began packing our bags to set off for our next port of call in Arizona. We had much enjoyed San Francisco, and everyone had been most kind and helpful and extremely polite. All nations under the sun seemed to be sitting in the open air at eating places, watching everyone go by.

We had a change of plan then, as we had decided we couldn't face another 36 hours on a Greyhound bus so we were taken to the airport early in the morning by the Woottons and our plane took off for Tucson, a town not all that far from the Mexican border. We travelled by Pacific South West Airline, and stopped at San Diego and Phoenix before arriving at Tucson. We were met at the airport by Vera Andersen and her daughter Lydia. I had not seen Vera since leaving Milan in March 1946. She was then a member of the congregation at All Saints Milan, the church I was in charge of for the last nine months of my Army career. It was exciting seeing her and meeting her husband Walter. She is tremendous fun and very attractive, and we laughed so much it was really quite exhausting. Our welcome was fantastic and she had a welcome present for us, a lovely copper bowl, made from the copper that is mined here. Next morning we had all sorts of adventures in Tucson, too many to detail, and we were taken to see various interesting places, one of which was where the Indians had resided many hundreds of years ago.

One place had the name Tombstone, and at Tombstone we saw a cemetery with rocks stacked up in piles and marked with a wooden cross. The ground being too hard to dig, they had just covered the bodies with stones and rocks. All sorts were buried here, and especially victims of Indian Apache raids and of shoot-outs by local residents. Several were shot, some hanged and one grave bore the inscription, 'Hanged by mistake'! The whole graveyard looked as if it was straight out of a Wild West film except that this was real. Many Wild West films have been filmed in this place, and the old stores and barns with their wooden verandas and platforms, are still in everyday use. I found it quite fascinating, and it brought back memories of playing cowboys and Indians in ones childhood. The Indians now live in reservations, but many Indian names abound. Tombstone got its name from the fact that the first prospector was warned all he would ever get would be his own tomb and be killed by the Apache Indians. In fact he found silver here, and this place became a most flourishing settlement with a population of 10,000, but the silver only lasted ten years and now the population is quite small, but it is a fascinating place to visit.

We went with Vera, her husband and daughter to the Church of St Philip-in-the-Hills and it was quite lovely. The building is beautiful - the east end filled with plain glass so the congregation look straight out on to cactus plants, palm trees, mountains and blue sky in the distance, all as if we were outside, and it was so, so beautiful. The view of the mountains is like a scene from the Holy Land.

A marvellous experience to worship here, and the church was packed with people, with a large choir, and servers, and throbbing with life and the memory of it will remain with me always. In the afternoon we visited the Church of San Xavier, which is inside the Indian Reserve. This church has a style of architecture we had not seen before. Very plain on the outside but the inside is very ornate and typical of 'old fashioned' Roman Catholicism. This pure white building stands in the midst of the sands, sizzling in the sun.

One day we visited the United States National Observatory some 50 miles away from where Vera lives, in the Quinland Mountains and the Sonora Desert and an Indian Reservation. The observatory is 7,000 feet up and boasts the largest solar telescope in the world. It was interesting to see all the massive instruments and the technical machinery, and people come to see it from all over the world. The real joy for us was the journey to and fro. The road goes through the desert with wonderful colours of the mountains and rocks, desert flowers and vegetation. It's hard to describe and one has to say it is different and leave it at that. The observatory is perched high in the hills and for the last 12 miles before getting there, the road had very hilly hairpin bends and lovely panoramic views. It is such a wonderful drive with a marvellous view at the top.

One morning we went to the Colorado National Forest to see the Madeira Canyon. This winds through the mountains quite near Tucson and there's a special tram-like bus which takes one through the canyon and back again. It was another beautiful morning, and quite fresh and pleasant in the hills, and after lunch we drove to see an Arizonan ranch, 130 thousand acres in size and stocked by more than 2,000 cattle. Mentioning the size of the range and number of cattle it sounds as though it is a very large area and not many cattle, but each animal needs, they told me, some 60 acres in order to survive, such is the poor quality of the soil, mostly just desert scrub, and looking at it one wondered how the animals managed to survive at all. The cattle roam free and the cowboys have a piece of land 27 miles by 8 miles to look after, and all of them do their work on horseback. The farmer was a real western American type with a large Stetson hat, and also very delightful. It was an interesting experience and once again very different from anything one would see in England.

The following day we got up at the crack of dawn and left at 6 o'clock in the morning to go on a trip to the Grand Canyon, one of the great wonders of the world. We travelled by coach, and went via the towns of Phoenix and Flagstaff and visited a place called Monteguma on the way. This is an Indian settlement built within caves high on the side of the mountain and dating back thousands of years. All kinds of ornaments and tools were found here and are now on show, and it gives one an idea of the primitive existence going on all those years ago.

Eventually we arrived at the Grand Canyon village and had our first glimpse of this incredible natural phenomenon. Everyone has heard about it, and now we were here actually looking at it. An awe inspiring and breathtaking experience. It is the largest in the world, 217 miles long, 18 miles wide and over 1 mile deep, with the Colorado River running through the bottom. It really is not possible to describe it. It has multi-coloured rocks in amazing formation, so that it looks as if it has been hand carved. We walked round and watched the changing colours and the setting sun, and finally made our way to our hotel. The accommodation is owned by the United States Government, and is exceedingly well done. Our room was large and airy, and well fitted out and with a private bath.

We went to bed early in order to make the most of the next day. We got up at six and were walking round the rim of the Canyon by 6.45, and returned for breakfast at 8 o'clock. After breakfast we caught the Shuttle, which is a kind of tram-like bus, and it runs along the rim of the canyon (now an American National Park), stopping at various viewpoints as it goes, and there's a commentary given by the driver, so everything is provided and there's no charge. We went to the end of the route, got off and walked back to the next point then got a shuttle again, got off and on again and finally finished on foot. The shuttle service, which runs every 15 minutes in both directions, really is good and one can get on and off as and when the mood takes one.

We had to bring to an end the Grand Canyon tour and journey back to Tucson, and what a magnificent journey it was. The road runs all through the mountains and pine forests, eventually coming right down through Oak Tree Canyon and Sedonia, and if the Grand Canyon is amazing in its size and colour, Oak Tree Canyon surpasses all. The rock formations, the trees, the running water, defy description. This is quite the best thing I have ever seen or experienced, and we much enjoyed the rest of the journey home through the mountains, watching the lovely colours of the sunset until darkness fell. We got back to Tucson late at night, very tired but after a memorable expedition. The round trip had covered more than 700 miles, so we saw quite a lot of Arizona!

Another thing we did was travel to the border town

of Nogale on the Mexican border. Here everyone spoke Spanish, and the road signs and shop notices were in that language. The people were dark skinned, much more so than I had expected, and the children with their dark hair and complexion looked very attractive. In early times the whole of this area was under Spanish control before being purchased by the American Government and incorporated into the United States. On the way home we visited the remains of the Tumacascori Mission. In 1691 a Jesuit Priest from Spain set up a mission in this part of this world but in 1767 the Jesuits were expelled from all Spanish dominions and the Franciscans took over the mission train in Sonora.

The Indians who lived here were friendly, except for the Apache, and these were continually raiding the mission. One can still see the ruins of the church which was begun in 1801, but by 1848 Apache raids made life impossible so the place was abandoned and everything possible taken to San Xavier near Tucson. The buildings were raided for treasure and gradually ruined, but in 1921 repair work was carried out and the United States Government now cares for the buildings. There is a very good collection of mementoes from the past. I have vague memories of reading about the Spanish and Jesuit Missions in the 17th / 18th Century, and this visit acted as an incentive to reread American/Mexican history.

On our second Sunday we went to St Philips-in-the Hills again, and as on the previous week much enjoyed sharing in the service in this lovely church. Our thoughts flew back to Blendworth, Chalton and Idsworth, and I remembered it was now about 6.30 pm in England, so all the morning services had long since finished. Wherever we went, the Church of England seemed very much alive and kicking.

On our last day in Tucson and Arizona we had to spend our time packing our bags and saying our farewells before moving off again. Our holiday fell into six sections: 1) Bedford and Nova Scotia, 2) Toronto and Orangeville, 3) the great train journey through the Rocky Mountains, 4) Vancouver, Victoria Island and British Columbia. 5) San Francisco and its environs, then 6) Tucson in Arizona and finally our return to Nova Scotia and home. Vera, Walter and Lydia saw us off from Tucson Airport and our plane left for Chicago where we changed planes and flew off to Halifax to stay once with Sue and Roger in Bedford, Nova Scotia.

For our last day it was raining and blowing and generally unpleasant, so it was a good help in getting us used to the idea of coming back to the English climate, the weather was like any day as it might have been in England in March or April. We flew home during the night and arrived at Heathrow at 9am. Our watches said it was 5am, so we were somewhat sleepy when we collected our luggage and were met by our son James, and headed home to Rowlands Castle having been away for just over six weeks. Each section of the holiday was quite different from that which went before, and it was really not possible to make comparisons.

Everywhere we received marvellous hospitality and generosity. We were much impressed by the kindness and helpfulness of the shop assistants and the like, and we revised our ideas about America and Americans quite a bit. Our preconceived notions were based on what we had seen and heard on films and television, and from the occasional contact during the war or with visitors coming to this country. We found everyone quiet, unobtrusive and courteous. We visited many restaurants and public places and found everything clean and wholesome, and the food and service very good indeed. Nowhere did we come across the brashness so often associated with Americans. It's true we visited only the west and south and it may be different elsewhere, but I have no recollection of seeing a policeman anywhere at any time, though no doubt there were some. All in all we were most impressed and thoroughly enjoyed our adventures.

After this wonderful trip to Canada and America there were other holidays, and we visited Egypt, the Holy Land, and various parts of Europe. Our visit to Czechoslovakia brought us up against the then Communist Regime, and it showed us a country where electricity was in very short supply, so the trams ran at night time with no lights on, and the vestibules of hotels and shop windows were all in darkness. Prices everywhere were stabilised and the local inhabitants were not allowed to take money out of the country. This meant they were constantly trying to get hold of English pounds. We asked our courier, "Are there any concentration camps in Czechoslovakia?" and he replied, "Czechoslovakia is one big concentration camp". Things of course in that part of the world have changed dramatically since then.

At the time of the attack on the Twin Towers in America, Muriel suddenly collapsed, and after a brain scan it was found part of it had been affected by a mini stroke, and she who had been a wonderful cook and excellent housekeeper, wife and mother could no longer cope with the cooking and the shopping and the general business of living. For about a year we lived on 'Farm Foods', which were delivered to the door and then heated up in the oven. Very good, but never quite the same as mother used to make.

We were sad we had to decide to leave our bungalow and the neighbourhood and take up residence in Abbeyfield House in Westbourne where food and care are provided. Abbeyfield House was well known to me from the time I first took an interregnum at Westbourne Parish Church. At that time I conducted a service of Holy Communion in the dining room once a month, and also attended various functions there, so I knew the staff and committee who ran it very well. Much needed care and attention was given to Muriel and she managed with the aid of a walking frame. She used to descend to the dining room in the lift and I carried her walking frame downstairs and waited at the bottom for her, and then we did it in reverse, she going up in the lift and I carrying the frame upstairs. Gradually she needed more and more care and attention, and Margaret, the warden, proved a wonderful help during this difficult part of our lives. Without her assistance it would have been impossible for us to stay as long as we did. What she did for us far exceeded the call of official duty and she deserves to be remembered for her kindness to us and other residents.

Muriel 1945

Eventually, however, Margaret said it was no longer possible for Muriel to stay, as her health continued to deteriorate, so we were faced with the problem once more of what to do next.

At this point Muriel was taken very ill, and spent two weeks in St Mary's Hospital in Portsmouth. When she was discharged she went direct to Springfield Nursing Home, which is roughly between Emsworth and Havant. She had stayed there some time before, because when I went in to Haslar Hospital to undergo an operation for a new knee, she stayed for the time I was in hospital and the time I was convalescent, so it now seemed the best place for her. Thus began for me several months of a daily visit to the Nursing Home, returning to Abbeyfield to spend the rest of the day on my own.

I was persuaded to give up driving my car on my 94th birthday and the good folk of Westbourne Parish Church organised a rota of people willing to take me to and fro to church and other events. After some months, when the chance of sharing a double room at Springfield came our way, I decided I would move from Abbeyfield into the Nursing Home and we shared accommodation there. The Matron and all the staff were extremely kind and did everything possible to make us happy and be well looked after.

Through the kindness of members of the congregation I was able to continue attending services at Westbourne on Sundays and weekdays, but Muriel was unable to come with me. She found this hard to accept and continually expressed sadness because of it. Very understandable, of course, because for 60 years we had done everything together. So it was that when an offer of accommodation came up at Manormead at Hindhead, where there is a chapel and other amenities, and extensive grounds, and I knew Muriel would be able to attend chapel services, we decided to move.

It was a difficult decision to make, because we had lived in that part of the world, at Blendworth, Rowlands Castle and Westbourne for 37 years, and had belonged to Westbourne Church for over 25 of them. We did not wish to leave our friends and neighbours, but it seemed right to move and in August 2007 we entered Manormead, where we had a delightful double room with a lovely view of the garden, adjacent to the chapel and other amenities. Muriel received wonderful nursing care, though our stay together proved to be quite short because she became steadily more frail and died on the 9th December 2007, just over three months after we moved. Her funeral took place at Westbourne and was a wonderful occasion, with the church full of friends and families, and the service taken by the Rector Richard Wells.

Muriel as a child lived in Carshalton in Surrey, and was one of nine children, all of them brought up as faithful Christians and all remained so for the rest of their lives. When she left school, a boarding school near Nottingham, she went to Paris for two years and lived with a wealthy family as companion to their teenage daughter. She studied French at the Sorbonne and was very warmly welcomed at the English Church of St George in Paris where she worshipped each Sunday. On her return to England she was employed by the Swiss Bank Corporation in the City of London and she was working there until the outbreak of war. In 1938 when war seemed inevitable she joined the Red Cross to train as a Nurse, and at the outbreak of war on September 3rd 1939 was immediately called up as a VAD nurse and served for six years. Her nursing service took her to Woolwich in London, Bournemouth, Netley near Southampton, the Isle of Wight and then finished overseas.

In 1944 volunteers were asked for service overseas. Muriel volunteered and was sent to 103 General Hospital situated south of Naples in Italy. Here she met the Chaplain of the Hospital whom she married in 1946! When the war ended Muriel returned to England and rejoined the Swiss Bank Corporation, remaining there while waiting for her fiancé to come home from Italy. On his return, we were married in St Matthew's Church at the Elephant and Castle, London on April 2nd 1946, and soon after I was instituted Vicar of St Philip, Lambeth. So began a wonderful partnership. Muriel was, for me, the ideal vicar's wife, entering fully into the life of the parish and enabling me to do all kinds of jobs in many helpful ways.

Our children Andrew, Timothy, Rachel and James, and our grandchildren were very dear to her, and she never ceased to be concerned for their welfare. She had a sunny nature, and would sing as she did her housework and cooking, rushing here and there, being energetic and loving holidays at home and abroad, walking at a great pace and always wanting more. In latter days it was sad to see her decline in health, so unlike her old self.

Much of what I did would not have been possible without the help of Muriel, and our joint ministry, as it can be called, lasted nearly 62 years. We've been much blessed and are grateful for everything. The local Doctor GP says, "I will always remember Muriel as a vibrant and dynamic person and a kind neighbour. Muriel was a lovely lady and is sadly missed."

Muriel and I had a long, enjoyable and fulfilling life

together, and no one could ask for more. We are grateful to all who have helped us on the way, and I am grateful for the privilege of serving God and his church in the sacred ministry. My life is now getting on for nearly 100 years and I have had many experiences and happy adventures. No doubt many failures as well as successes, but altogether a life which leaves me full of thankfulness and praise for the grace of God and the companionship of family and friends. There is much I have forgotten, but one extraordinary thing I must mention concerns the figure 2. I was born on the 22nd April, Muriel was born on the 2nd September. We were married on the 2nd and engaged on the 2nd. Andrew was born on the 2nd and Timothy, our second son, was born on the 2nd and his initials spell TWO. Queenie my sister died in 1922, I began theological studies in 1932, went abroad with the Army in 1942, became vicar of St Andrews, Surbiton in 1952, and vicar of the Ascension, Balham in 1962 and we found ourselves living at No 22. When we retired to the bungalow in Rowlands Castle, we found it was called Two Willows - all very extraordinary coincidences.

I end these memories of Here and There with a quotation written by Michael Mayne, former Dean of Westminster:

"If atheists are right and I am proved wrong, if my deepest beliefs are what many describe as mere fairytales, if there is nothing at the end, then I shall still not have wished to have lived in any other way or to have based this one precious life on any other facts. Despite all the darknesses they have not only brought much joy but I can think of nothing else that would have satisfied my deepest desires, convictions and hopes."

Archbishop of Canterbury at Manormead, 2008

ARCHBISHOP OF CANTERBURY

The Revd Canon H G Ockwell
Springfield
74 Havant Road
Emsworth
Hampshire PO10 7LH

24 June 2007

Dear Canon Ockwell,

News that you are about to celebrate an astonishing seventy years of ordination has reached Lambeth Palace, and I wanted to write and express on behalf of the whole Church what St John's Westbourne already feels so deeply – our deep and abiding sense of gratitude for the faithfulness of your ministry through so many years of priestly service. In that ordination service in 1937, after examining your resolve, the bishop said, 'Almighty God who hath given you this will to do all these things, grant also unto you strength and power to perform the same that he may accomplish his work which he hath begun in you.' God may truly be thanked for keeping his word all these years – to you, and through you to so many others.

Every blessing & good wish,

+ Rowan Cantuar:

Lambeth Palace, London SE1 7JU

Printed in the United Kingdom by
Lightning Source UK Ltd., Milton Keynes
139712UK00001B/43/P